Praise for *Reviving Old Scratch*

"In a world where it's awkward to talk about spiritual warfare, Richard Beck reminds us why it's still necessary, and he gives us words, images, and stories to start the conversation. Let him (re)introduce you to the devil!"

—Sara Barton
Chaplain at Pepperdine University and
author of *A Woman Called*

"I'm grateful to Richard Beck for helping us reclaim that which was clearly important to Jesus: casting out demons and contending with evil. While I'm not sure if I *believe* in spiritual warfare, I'm certain I've *experienced* it, and *Reviving Old Scratch* allowed me to come several steps closer to reconciling these seemingly irreconcilable statements. Beck manages to take demons, the devil, and spiritual warfare and pull them into the reality we live in today and for that I am grateful."

—Nadia Bolz-Weber
Author of *Pastrix* and *Accidental Saints*
and pastor of House for All Sinners and Saints

"In our secular age, most western Christians instinctively dismiss the devil and demons as antiquated mythical notions of our superstitious past. Yet, as Richard Beck argues, this dismissal adversely affects both the coherence and the vibrancy of the Christian faith. In this insightful and highly important masterpiece, Beck helps Christians understand that they need not suspend their doubts about "Old Scratch" to discern his reality in the dark dehumanizing forces that are all around us. Whether you're convinced or doubtful of Satan's existence, this book will inspire you to enter into the age-long spiritual battle that has always been at the center of the Christian faith."

—Gregory A. Boyd
Author of *God at War* and *Satan and the Problem of Evil*

"Richard Beck is one of the most important and fascinating minds in contemporary Christianity, and this exploration on the devil and demons is his best work yet. Lively, engaging, and profoundly relevant, *Reviving Old Scratch* manages to both tickle and challenge, inform and delight. Beck forges a fresh way forward that avoids the conservative tendency to overspiritualize the devil and demons on the one hand and the progressive tendency to reduce these powerful forces to social issues on the other. A must-read for skeptics and thinkers, *Reviving Old Scratch* surprises in all the right ways. I couldn't put it down!"

—Rachel Held Evans
Author of *Searching for Sunday* and
A Year of Biblical Womanhood

"Richard Beck's *Reviving Old Scratch* will first put your theory of Satan and demons and the powers to death, then it will make you wonder if there isn't more than social justice and activism and believing in real, personal demons and angels, and then it will put a real Old Scratch with a mask onto what you thought was dead, and then you will be armed for the deeper battles of life and justice and love. Beck's prison ministry with people who suffer at the hands of Old Scratch evokes authentic spirituality in a way no other book about the powers has done. #thinkagain"

—Scot McKnight
Northern Seminary

"Profound and compelling. Follow Richard Beck as he narrates the interconnection between spiritual warfare and social justice through the powers and principalities. I highly recommend it!"

—Kyle Strobel
Professor of spiritual theology at Biola University and
co-author of *The Way of the Dragon or the Way of the Lamb:
Searching for Jesus' Path of Power in a
Church that has Abandoned It*

REVIVING OLD SCRATCH

REVIVING OLD SCRATCH

DEMONS AND THE DEVIL
∼ FOR ∼
DOUBTERS AND THE DISENCHANTED

Richard Beck

Fortress Press
Minneapolis

REVIVING OLD SCRATCH
Demons and the Devil for Doubters and the Disenchanted

Cover design: Brad Norr
Interior design and typesetting: PerfecType, Nashville, TN

Library of Congress Cataloging-in-Publication Data
Print ISBN: 978-1-5064-0135-5
eBook ISBN: 978-1-5064-0136-2

The paper used in this publication meets the minimum requirements of American National Standard for Information Sciences — Permanence of Paper for Printed Library Materials, ANSI Z329.48-1984.

Manufactured in the U.S.A.

For the Men in White and the saints at Freedom Fellowship

I have found, in short, from reading my own writing, that my subject in fiction is the action of grace in territory largely held by the devil.

I have also found that what I write is read by an audience which puts little stock either in grace or the devil.
—Flannery O'Connor

If this life is not a real fight, in which something is eternally gained for the universe by success, it is no better than a game of private theatricals from which one may withdraw at will. But it feels like a real fight.
—William James

The reason the Son of God appeared was to destroy the devil's work.
—1 John 3:8

TABLE OF CONTENTS

Introduction: Old Scratch. xiii

Part 1: Wickedness in High Places: Spiritual Warfare as Social Justice

Chapter 1: Still Prowling the World 3

Chapter 2: Scooby-Doo, Where Are You! 13

Part 2: To Destroy the Devil's Work: Spiritual Warfare beyond Social Justice

Chapter 3: Jesus the Exorcist 29

Chapter 4: The White Witch. 39

Chapter 5: Holy Ghost Conga Lines. 49

Chapter 6: The Wizard of Oz 57

Chapter 7: I Love Humanity. It's People I Can't Stand! 67

Chapter 8: God at War. 79

Part 3: A Great Campaign of Sabotage: Spiritual Warfare for Doubters and the Disenchanted

Chapter 9: "Get Behind Me, Satan!" 87

Chapter 10: The War of the Lamb 95

Chapter 11: Angels and Demons 103

Chapter 12: Resist the Devil 119

Chapter 13: The Lucifer Effect 133

Chapter 14: The One Who Holds the Power of Death 145

Chapter 15: Turning the World Upside Down 161

Chapter 16: Satan Interrupted 171

Epilogue: A Prison Story 185

Acknowledgments 191

INTRODUCTION: OLD SCRATCH

On Monday nights you'll find me in prison.

From 6:30 to 8:30 every Monday evening, my friend Herb Patterson and I lead a Bible study for about fifty inmates at the maximum-security French-Robertson Unit, just north of Abilene, Texas. After greeting the "Men in White" (inmates in Texas prisons wear all white) with hugs and small talk, during which I get to practice rudimentary Spanish greetings with the Hispanic men, we start the study with a prayer. Herb usually leads it.

A few years ago in the middle of his prayer Herb made a petition. "And Lord, protect us from Old Scratch . . ."

This caught my attention. Old Scratch? Who was Old Scratch? What was Herb talking about?

As soon as the prayer ended and we all lifted our heads, I asked aloud, "Herb, who is Old Scratch?"

Herb was incredulous. How was it possible that I didn't know who Old Scratch was? But looking around the room, none of the men in the study seemed to know who Old Scratch was either. We were all in the dark.

So Herb explained, "Old Scratch is the Devil."

I later learned that Old Scratch, as a colloquialism for the Devil, was a nickname that originated in England and was common in the last century in New England and the Southern United States.

Herb is a generation older than I am, and he grew up in the South, so during his childhood he regularly heard the Devil called "Old Scratch." Some think that the name Old Scratch originated from the Old Norse word *skratte* referring to a wizard or goblin. Attentive readers of literature might recall encountering Old Scratch in Mark Twain's *The Adventures of Tom Sawyer.* Aunt Polly describes Tom Sawyer as being "full of the Old Scratch" because of Tom's rebellious and mischievous ways. And in Charles Dickens's *A Christmas Carol*, during the visions of the Ghost of Christmas Yet to Come, Scrooge overhears a conversation describing his death: "Old Scratch has got his own at last."

This is a book about Old Scratch. More specifically, this is a book about what some Christians call "spiritual warfare," about what it might mean to "do battle" with the Devil. As we know, the Bible is full of admonitions about how to deal with Old Scratch:

"Get behind me, Satan!"

"Resist the Devil and he will flee from you."

"Watch out! Your enemy the devil prowls around like a roaring lion looking for someone to devour."

"Take up the shield of faith, with which you can extinguish all the flaming arrows of the evil one."

And in what is perhaps ground zero for all spiritual warfare talk, the Book of Ephesians, chapter six and verse twelve, in the grand tones of the King James Version:

"For we wrestle not against flesh and blood, but against principalities, against powers, against the rulers of the darkness of this world, against spiritual wickedness in high places."

So watch out for Old Scratch!

Which is why Herb prayed the prayer that he did.

But here's the problem: the Devil has fallen on hard times. Not in TV shows or Hollywood movies—our screens are still filled with stories of the Devil and demon possession. From the classic *The Exorcist* to the recent spat of *Paranormal Activity* films, as a cultural icon Old Scratch is still very much with us.

But the Devil as an object of belief? Not so much. More and more, Christians, to say nothing about our increasingly secular society, just don't believe in the Devil, at least not in any personal or literal sense.

For example, a 2009 survey conducted by the Barna Group found that 40 percent of the Christians surveyed strongly agreed with the statement that the Devil "is not a living being but is a symbol of evil." That's right, four out of ten Christians don't believe in the Devil. And an additional two of ten Christians surveyed said that they "somewhat agree" that the Devil isn't a literal being. Another 8 percent said they weren't sure.[1]

If you're keeping score, those results suggest that the *majority* of Christians don't believe in the literal existence of the Devil.

What's happened to Old Scratch?

The reasons, I think, are pretty obvious.

We're living in an increasingly modern, scientific, technological, and therefore more *skeptical* age. Faith is harder for us. Doubt fills our pews. And books about living with doubt fill the shelves of Christian bookstores. Many Christians are losing their belief in God, so when you look at the To-Do List of Belief, endorsing the existence of the Prince of Darkness seems pretty far down the list. To say nothing about spooky things like demon possession. When it comes to faith, we've got bigger fish to fry.

And talking about the Devil is more and more awkward and embarrassing these days—talking about demons around the workplace water-cooler is like telling a story about ghosts, alien abductions, or Bigfoot. It sounds crazy.

We're living in what Charles Taylor calls a "secular age," and this secular age is "disenchanted."[2] Our ancestors, by contrast, lived

---

1. "Most American Christians Do Not Believe That Satan or the Holy Spirit Exist." Barna Group. Web. 11 Dec. 2015.
2. Charles Taylor, *A Secular Age* (Cambridge, MA: Belknap of Harvard University Press, 2007).

in an "enchanted" world—and this was the world of the Bible—a world filled with magic, spirits, and supernatural powers. The Devil makes sense in an enchanted world.

But less so in our world. Science, technology, and electrical lighting have illuminated the dark, superstitious corners of our world, banishing all that was occult and spooky. Our secular age is *dis*-enchanted—full of wonder and awe, to be sure, but no longer spooky. Like the surveys point out, it's harder for us to believe in Old Scratch.

Doubt and disenchantment isn't the only problem with talking about Old Scratch. We also worry about harm. Many liberal and progressive Christians, from the mainline Protestant traditions to post-fundamentalist Christians, have left the church of their youth in search of a more loving, inclusive, and intellectually respectable Christianity. And they worry about the potential for abuse and demonization when Christians talk about the Devil and demons. People have been psychologically scarred by abusive deliverance ministries or by churches where deliverance and exorcism are regularly practiced. It can mess with your head to be told you've been possessed by demons, and far too often the language of spiritual warfare has been used to demonize other human beings.

The trouble with the Devil is that we see him in the faces of those we hate, justifying our violence toward them. We don't need to rehash this long and dark history, for we all know how the Devil has been used to scapegoat despised and marginalized groups. We always smell sulfur around those we wish to kill.

Having seen "spiritual warfare" used over and over as a tool of hatred and abuse, we want to put as much distance between ourselves and Old Scratch as possible. In the hands of human beings, talk about the Devil or spiritual warfare is just too dangerous. So let's keep our focus on the love, mercy, and grace of God, we think. When it comes to the Devil, prudence and the weight of Christian history suggest that it's best to just keep our mouths shut.

And lastly, to put the point rather bluntly, given our doubts and disenchantment the Devil just seems irrelevant to many of us, especially if our main job is to love other people. You don't need to believe in demon possession to practice the Golden Rule. You don't need to believe in spooky stuff to be a good person, let alone a good Christian.

And so you can, perhaps, appreciate the predicament of this book. Here is a book about Old Scratch for an audience who doesn't believe in the Devil and who thinks it would be best to avoid any talk about him.

And yet, here we are. This *is* a book about Old Scratch, and unapologetically so, a book about spiritual warfare written for a skeptical and worried audience. That's because I think it is absolutely essential that doubting and disenchanted Christians recover and invest in a theology of spiritual warfare. We need to talk more about Old Scratch. A lot more. I hope to show you why. But we've lost the ability to talk about the Devil. Or never had it in the first place. So introductions seem to be in order.

I'd like to introduce you to Old Scratch.

Now to be fair, doubting and disenchanted Christians haven't wholly ignored the Devil or the topic of spiritual warfare. We all know how often the Bible talks about the Devil. And while that spooky stuff might make the Bible awkward in light of our doubts, we feel obligated to do *something* with all that talk about the Devil and demons in Scripture. Consequently, in Part 1 of this book I will describe how many Christians have tended to approach the subject of spiritual warfare in light of their doubts and worries. These Christians, and I count myself among them, tend to create a very justice-oriented and politicized vision of spiritual warfare, all with good biblical justification. Our battle, to quote Ephesians 6 again, is against "the principalities and powers," and we take these powers to be the systemic forces of oppression and injustice in the world. In the hands of many doubting and disenchanted Christians, *spiritual warfare*—battling against the forces of darkness in the world—is synonymous with *social justice*.

And these insights will be critically important for readers who *do* believe in Old Scratch but who think about spiritual warfare almost exclusively terms of demon possession and exorcism. As I hope to show you, that narrow focus on possession and exorcism misses the heart of our battle with the Devil as it is described in the Bible.

There's a whole lot in the Bible that backs up the connection between spiritual warfare and social justice. And yet, there are problems here as well. When spiritual warfare is reduced to a political struggle for justice, a whole lot of other stuff gets left out. A lot of very important stuff. For example, a purely political vision of spiritual warfare often winds up in a very dark place. When we're fighting against oppressors in the world we have to remember the famous warning from Friedrich Nietzsche: "Beware that, when fighting monsters, you yourself do not become a monster." That's some of the irony with doubting and disenchanted Christians who refuse to talk about spiritual warfare because they worry it leads to dehumanization. Because Old Scratch, he's a slippery one! Dehumanization isn't so easy to avoid. As the Bible says, the Devil comes to us as an angel of light.

So in Part 2 we'll talk about all the reasons that a purely political vision of spiritual warfare is inadequate and often dangerous. I'll point out all the reasons why we need to start talking more about Old Scratch.

And that will bring us to Part 3, where I will (re-)introduce you to Old Scratch. I'll sketch out a way of talking about the Devil that will widen the view of those who do believe in the Devil as well as help doubting and disenchanted Christians get over our awkwardness in talking about Old Scratch. Because in our disenchanted age, getting over this awkwardness about the Devil seems to be our biggest obstacle, which is why I started this book with a story about the prison.

I learned to get over my awkwardness in talking about the Devil out at the prison. Caring as I do about injustices such as mass incarceration, capital punishment, and all the other problems related to our criminal justice system, my concerns about social justice brought me to the prison. But once I was *inside* the prison I quickly discovered that my disenchanted worldview clashed with the spirituality of the inmates who spoke about the Devil and demons all the time. Behind prison bars, Old Scratch is real as can be. And I had to figure out a way to make sense of it all.

The same thing happened to me when I joined Freedom Fellowship. Freedom is a faith community in one of the poorest parts of my town. We feed the hungry and share life on the margins of society. Members at Freedom are very poor, often homeless. Many struggle with psychiatric illness or cognitive disabilities. Many are fighting a battle with addiction, bouncing back and forth from rehab. And you often find members at Freedom wearing ankle monitors because they are on parole.

From the outside, the demographics of Freedom tell a grim story. But on the inside? Inside the walls of Freedom I've encountered a life-giving, joy-filled, charismatic, and Spirit-filled faith community. At Freedom we dance in the aisles, anoint with oil, and raise hands in worship. And we talk a whole lot about Old Scratch.

It's the exact same thing that happened to me out at the prison. I was attracted to Freedom because of my passion for social justice: I wanted to feed the hungry, clothe the naked, and shelter the homeless. And we do all those things at Freedom. But just like out at the prison, I encountered a charismatic spirituality at Freedom that didn't ignore the Devil. There I was, a doubting and disenchanted Christian, surrounded by talk of Old Scratch.

At Freedom and out at the prison I still struggle with my doubts, but if I wanted to share life there on the margins of my town, I knew I had to figure out a way to talk and think about the Devil in a way that wasn't ironic or fake. I didn't want to talk about Old Scratch with a knowing wink and my fingers crossed. And if you want to share life on the margins, you're going to have to figure this out as well.

My ambition for this book is very simple. I want to reintroduce you to Old Scratch. In our secular age we've lost our ability to talk about the Devil, and lots of things have been lost or gone wrong because of that. Despite all our doubts, we need to recover a vision of spiritual warfare.

We're all a bit skeptical, and our doubts and disenchantment won't wholly go away, but it's my hope that by the end of this book you could join me for prayer out at the prison on Monday nights. My hope is that you'd be able to sit among the Men in White to listen to Herb pray—"And Lord, protect us from Old Scratch"—and respond with a sincere and passionate "Amen!"

PART 1

Wickedness in High Places

Spiritual Warfare as Social Justice

Chapter 1

Still Prowling the World

"YOU'D LIKE FOR me to perform an exorcism? On your *wife*?"

The gentleman seated before me nodded solemnly.

And I had a bit of explaining to do.

I was doing a series of classes at a conference, sharing some of the material I was planning to use in this book. People attending the conference came to my class to hear about "spiritual warfare for doubters and the disenchanted," a class for Christians who were finding it increasingly awkward or difficult to talk about the Devil and spiritual warfare.

The gentleman asking me to perform an exorcism on his wife had missed that part of the title and class description. All he'd seen in the title were the words "spiritual warfare." And he'd assumed since I was teaching about "spiritual warfare" I would be someone who knew a thing or two about exorcism. So he had approached me to share some marital struggles along with a request to cast out an evil spirit from his wife.

Awkwardly, I explained to this man, who seemed legitimately distraught, that my class about spiritual warfare was for people who weren't all that sure the Devil existed, at least not in a literal, personal sense, that the class was for people who doubted that spiritual warfare involved things like, well, things like spousal exorcisms.

"So, you can't help me?" the man asked, slowly comprehending. "No sir," I said, "not in that way. But I can pray for you and your wife. Can I do that for you?" He agreed. I laid my hand on his shoulder and prayed for him, his wife, and their marriage. When I'd finished my prayer he looked up at me with tears in his eyes. "Thank you," he said, clearly moved. I was moved too. I hadn't been able to perform an exorcism, but I'd done what I could. And it seemed to help.

When you tell people you're writing a book about the Devil you find yourself in a lot of strange and awkward conversations. As you can imagine, people have shared with me some pretty wild stuff. And while I don't dismiss any of those stories, I do think it would be helpful here at the start to say a few things about the audience I have in mind for this book, along with how we'll be talking about the Devil. If just to avoid future requests for spousal exorcisms.

I have written this book mainly for Christians who have a lot of questions and doubts about things like demon possession and exorcism. These doubting and disenchanted Christians often describe themselves with a bewildering array of labels—labels such as liberal, progressive, emergent, post-fundamentalist, or post-evangelical. A common thread running through these labels is an eagerness to embrace science, a faith that unapologetically embraces the current scientific consensus in biology, geology, cosmology, and every other scientific discipline.

Now, a scientifically educated and sophisticated faith is a wonderful thing, but scientific literacy has a price. Embracing science can cause us to doubt the spookier aspects of faith. Science can increase our disenchantment, making beliefs in angels, demons, and exorcisms seem superstitious and quaint, like a retreat to the Dark Ages when we burned witches and thought the sun revolved around the earth.

So faith is affected by an embrace of science, but doubts and disenchantment aren't the only things that characterize liberal and progressive Christians. Beyond scientific literacy, progressive and liberal Christians tend to cultivate a socially conscious and politically engaged faith focused upon fighting injustices in the world. And there's a reason these two things—scientific literacy and social consciousness—go hand-in-hand among liberal and progressive Christians: when you struggle with doubts and disenchantment concerning the supernatural, your faith becomes focused upon the world you can see and touch, the earth and all her inhabitants. By increasing our focus on the material *earth*, rather than on unseen *heaven*, doubt and disenchantment push us toward more ecologically and socially conscious expressions of faith. Consequently, when it comes to a subject like spiritual warfare, the spookier elements of evil are traded in for evils that can be seen and physically rectified. For instance, you might harbor doubts about demon possession, but you can dig a well in Africa so that a village can have access to clean drinking water. You may not believe in evil spirits, but you can fight the evil of sex trafficking. You may not know what it means to "resist the Devil," but you can resist economic systems that exploit the poor.

You get the idea. There's plenty of evil to go around, so if you doubt supernatural and spooky evil, it's not like you're left twiddling your thumbs. You've still got plenty of work to do in the world.

That's the main audience I have in mind for this book. I wrote this book for doubting and disenchanted Christians who find it hard, awkward, or silly to talk about things like the Devil or spiritual warfare and who tend to see their fight against evil as the political fight for justice in the world. I embrace that vision of justice, but I'm also going to explain why it's important for these Christians to start talking more about Old Scratch.

A Little Improv

Of course, liberal and progressive Christians aren't the only Christians concerned about social justice, oppression, poverty, violence, and economic exploitation. And if the surveys are correct that the majority of Christians doubt the literal existence of the Devil, progressive Christians aren't the only believers who bring some skepticism into any conversation about the Devil and spiritual warfare. So while I have a particular reader in mind for this book I'm also casting a very wide net.

And to cast the net even wider I want to say a few more things to readers who actually do believe in demon possession and exorcism, readers who don't struggle with doubts or disenchantment. Can a book like this—a "Devil for Doubters" book—be of any use to that man who asked me to perform an exorcism?

Oh yes it can!

A lot Christians who believe in the Devil tend to think that spiritual warfare is almost exclusively about demon possession and exorcism. But as I hope to show you, that vision of spiritual warfare has more to do with Hollywood movies than the battle we see between Jesus and Satan in the Bible. When it comes to the Devil, if you're thinking primarily about possession and exorcism you need to widen your view.

To help you do that, let me make a suggestion. When it comes to thinking about faith, I'm a big believer in the fundamental rule of comedy improv: *Yes, and.* When you're in an improv scene and your partner gives you a premise—"Ouch, my head hurts!"—you don't block her with a negation: "No it doesn't. Your head doesn't hurt." Blocking—leading with a *No*—kills the whole scene. Leading with a *No* drains the forward momentum, and the scene has nowhere to go. So the Golden Rule of Improv is: *Yes, and.* You lead with *Yes*, you lead with affirmation. But you don't end there. You don't merely agree. "Yes, I wholeheartedly concur, your head hurts." That doesn't help either. The *Yes* must be followed by an *and*. You add your own premise to move the scene forward. "Ouch, my head hurts!" your improv partner says, rubbing her head. In response you wag your finger and adopt a scolding tone, "How many times have I warned you that riding elephants is dangerous!" You've affirmed your partner and have added your own twist, handing back to her something more to work with. No longer blocked by *No*, a whole world opens up before you and the audience, a world to discover and explore for the enjoyment of all. Why were you riding elephants that day? Everyone wants to know!

Yes, and. For readers who believe in demons and exorcism, that's the posture I'd like for you to have as you read this book. There's no need to pick and choose between different visions of spiritual warfare. This isn't a contest or a debate. No need for a blocking *No*. Yes, you might think there is something *more* that needs to be said about spiritual warfare. That's great. Just add that to the mix. *Yes, and.* But this book will expand and enrich, theologically and biblically, how you think about the Devil, demons, and spiritual warfare. Especially if all you think spiritual warfare involves is demon possession and exorcism. Again, that narrow focus is missing the most important lessons the Bible teaches us about tangling with Old Scratch. So I hope you'll be delighted, surprised, and deeply edified by what I have to share with you.

Naming the Devil

Finally, before we get into the thick of the book we need to get clear about what we are talking about when we make reference to the Devil and Satan.

If the surveys are to be believed, many Christians tend to think of the Devil as a "symbol of evil" rather than as a literal fallen angel. However, there are a couple of problems with thinking about the Devil as a "symbol of evil."

First, many might assume that *symbol* means *pretend* or *make-believe*. But symbols aren't pretend, they're pointing to something real, something happening in the world. So that's the first thing we need to get clear about. Fallen angel or symbol, the Devil is real.

Okay, great, the Devil is real. But what, exactly, are we naming in the world when we speak of the Devil? Here we want to stay close to the Bible because "symbol of evil" isn't the way the Bible describes Satan. The proper name "Satan" comes from the Hebrew *ha satan*, a word that simply means "adversary." Everyone can and has acted at some point as "a satan." Even God's actions are described as "satanic" in the Old Testament.[1] In the New Testament, Satan is also called *diabolos* translated as "devil," but also as "accuser" or "adversary."

Basically, a satan is more of a relationship than a person. Anything that is facing you in an antagonistic or adversarial way—working against you as an opponent or enemy—is standing before you as *ha satan*, as an adversary, as a satan. In the Bible, Satan and the Devil are interchangeable names for the personification of all that is adversarial to the kingdom and people of God, the personified Enemy of God.

Now, does "Satan" or "the Devil" name a literal, supernatural *person*, or does "Satan" name a symbolic *personification* of all the forces in the world antagonistic to the kingdom of God? Depending upon your doubts and disenchantment we could have a long conversation about that question. But for our purposes we simply need to agree on the biblical vision of Satan and the Devil. Biblically, Satan names that which is working against God and God's kingdom in the world.

Satanic Board Games (Non-Ouija Edition)

When I talk about Satan or the Devil in this book I'm pointing to that which is *adversarial to the kingdom of God*. And while Christians might disagree about the exact nature of the forces arrayed against

---

1. For example, see Numbers 22:22, when God sends an angel to block the path of the prophet Balaam (ESV): "But God's anger was kindled because he went, and the angel of the Lord took his stand in the way as his *adversary* [in Hebrew *satan*]." And yes, this the same Balaam of talking donkey fame.

the kingdom, we recognize these forces as real and active in the world, forces that need to be fought and resisted. That struggle and that fight is what I'm calling "spiritual warfare." In this book, "spiritual warfare" is shorthand for the Christ-shaped pushback against all the forces in the world working antagonistically against the kingdom of God.

Now everything—absolutely everything—in this conversation depends upon what we mean by "kingdom of God." Get that wrong and everything goes wrong, because you can't name a force as *adversarial* until you define what you're moving against and toward. It's *yin* and *yang*. You need to have a goal in mind before you name your obstacles and opponents—even if the game is *cooperative*, you're still going to run into a satan. It's called *conflict*.

For example, I've played a lot of cooperative board games with my family, games where players are not trying to beat each other, but work together. Unlike competitive "I Win/You Lose" games, like checkers or chess, cooperative games have a Win/Win dynamic, games like *Forbidden Island* where all the players work together to escape an island before it sinks into the ocean. But cooperation in games like *Forbidden Island* is no easy thing. That's the challenge of these games, why we like to test ourselves by playing them. To put it rather weirdly, there has to be a *satanic* aspect to the cooperative game, or we wouldn't play it. There are tons of dynamics working *against* our cooperation: ego, impatience, conflict over best strategies. We even have to forgive each other. That's what makes the games so challenging and rewarding, the fact that we had to *overcome* so much, that we had to *struggle* so hard to cooperate. And beyond the effort that it takes to work together, in these games, the players are struggling to overcome some impersonal and implacable force in the game that's working against the team, thwarting us from reaching our goals. When my family and I play *Forbidden Island* it's us, as a team, against that diabolical island.

All that to say, I understand that lots of us would rather avoid all this talk about satans, adversaries, and warfare. It all seems so dark and hostile. We'd much rather focus our faith on positive things, things like love, grace, and inclusion, but that's a deeply ironic and confused desire. Why can't we just focus on the *positive?* Because positive doesn't have any meaning without its *relationship* to something negative. The journey toward love doesn't make any sense without an associated struggle against hate. The heroism of mercy isn't heroic if there aren't temptations toward vengeance and revenge. A call for inclusion doesn't make any sense if no one is being excluded. It's simple logic. Fighting for justice assumes injustice. Protecting victims assumes people are being victimized.

Shall I say it again? *The Devil is real.*

I'd love to have a Christianity full of rainbows and daisies, full of love and inclusion. But there are forces working against love and inclusion in the world, and some of those forces are at work in my own heart and mind. We call those forces *hate* and *exclusion*, to say nothing about everything else that is tearing the world to shreds, pushing the loving and gracious rule of God out of the world.

Hate is the satan of love.

Exclusion is the satan of inclusion.

War is the satan of peace.

Oppression is the satan of justice.

Tearing down is the satan of building up.

Competition is the satan of cooperation.

Revenge is the satan of mercy.

Harm is the satan of care.

Hostility is the satan of reconciliation.

There is a satan to the kingdom of God.

If you follow Jesus, you know there is *anti*-Jesus. If you've read the Gospels you know Jesus was fighting a huge battle against formidable forces, forces that ultimately killed him—that's what I mean by *anti-Jesus.* And throughout that struggle—and this is the critical point can we can't ever, ever forget—Jesus never becomes anti-Jesus. Unlike us, Jesus never takes the bait, never becomes Satan to fight Satan. And repeatedly in the Gospels, Jesus pulls his followers away from becoming anti-Jesus. *Peter*, Jesus says in the garden of Geth-semane, *put your sword away*. All the way to the cross, Jesus stays Jesus. Jesus never returns evil for evil, violence for violence, curse for curse, blow for blow, eye for eye or tooth for tooth. Jesus never becomes anti-Jesus. And neither should we.

But if anything should convince a Christian that Satan exists—as person or personification—it has to be the crucifixion of Jesus. Something—something from the very start—was *against* Jesus. And the Bible calls that force Satan.

And that anti-Jesus force is still very much at work in the world—and in my own heart.

So, yes, by all means let's stay positive and keep focused on Jesus. Let's talk about love and grace. But let's also admit that we have to talk about Satan. We have to talk about what Jesus was fighting for. And against. And why he was killed.

There are forces adversarial to love and grace in the world, and I don't care all that much if you think those forces are due to Beel-zebub, a dark tendency of human psychology, or the Second Law of Thermodynamics. If God is love and if love is at the heart of the kingdom of God, that love is a heroic act of resistance in a world governed by hate, violence, and indifference.

Jesus, the exact representation of the invisible God, entered the world full of grace, mercy, and love. And for that he was tortured and crucified.

Does the Devil exist? As in *literally*?

I don't know. Maybe. I wouldn't rule it out. But I do know this:

Something killed Jesus. Something real. And the Bible named it:

Satan. The Devil. Old Scratch. The adversary to the kingdom of God.

And the Bible warns us that Satan is still out there, still prowl-ing the world, like a lion, looking for someone to devour.

Chapter 2

Scooby-Doo, Where Are You!

BACK IN THE day, I was a huge fan of the show *Scooby-Doo, Where Are You!* Scooby-Doo and the gang—Shaggy, Fred, Daphne, and Velma—were a highlight of Saturday-morning and after-school cartoon viewing. The sound and lyrics of Austin Roberts's iconic theme song for the show—*"Scooby-Dooby Doo, where are you! We've got some work to do now"*—had us running to the TV.

If you've never watched *Scooby-Doo*, particularly the early episodes, the plot of each episode followed a standard pattern: Scooby-Doo, a dog who can kind of talk, along with his four teenaged friends—members of the investigative team Mystery Inc. driving a psychedelically decorated van named the "Mystery Machine"—find themselves in a town plagued by a ghost, spook, monster, or otherwise supernatural creature. Scooby and the kids commence with an investigation, examining clues, and interviewing the townspeople. During the investigation the gang has scary encounters with the ghost or monster. Eventually the gang creates a trap for the creature, usually sprung at the end of a comedic and extended chase scene. Having captured the creature, Scooby-Doo and friends unmask the monster, revealing it to be not a monster or ghost but someone from the town who was using the creature to scare people away from noticing some sort of criminal activity. The show would often end with the unmasked crook going off to jail lamenting, "I would have gotten away with it, too, if it hadn't been for you meddling kids!"

In many ways, Scooby-Doo is a perfect parable of what it feels like to be a person of faith in a secular age, characterized by "disenchantment." In his book *A Secular Age*, Charles Taylor describes how over the last 500 years the Western world moved from enchantment to disenchantment.[1] Five hundred years ago the world was full of supernatural forces, witchcraft, monsters, and ghosts; the world was *enchanted*, rife with "thin places" where the borders between the material supernatural worlds touched; people could become demon possessed or cursed by witches; the night was full of occult menace and magic; black cats were bad luck.

Things are different today. We live in a skeptical age where science and technology define what is "true" and "real." With the advent of electric lighting, the dark forces that haunted the night have been banished. There's no room for monsters anymore. Paranormal reality shows on TV looking for ghosts or Bigfoot never find anything. Modern medicine and psychiatry diagnose schizophrenia rather than demon possession, and we seek out doctors rather than exorcists. Worrying about black cats is superstitious and irrational, and ghost stories are just that, stories—fictional tales to scare the kids around the campfire.

Any single episode of *Scooby-Doo* traces this 500-year trajectory, the movement in our lives from enchantment to disenchantment. The first part of a *Scooby-Doo* episode parallels the era of

---

1. Charles Taylor, *A Secular Age* (Cambridge, MA: Belknap of Harvard University Press, 2007).

enchantment, beginning as it does with a supernatural monster, ghoul, or ghost. But as the kids investigate, they grow suspicious and doubtful. As reason and evidence assert themselves, disenchantment grows and the supernatural creature—the agent of the occult—is eventually revealed to be Mr. Jenkins the greedy banker. A story that begins with enchantment ends with disenchantment. The supernatural was simply a cover for human greed, theft, and corruption.

Swimming Faithfully in a Sea of Disenchantment

Why do the majority of Christians doubt the literal existence of the Devil? We're affected by the pervasive skepticism and disenchantment of our "secular age," but it's not just that we're passively affected by our culture. A lot of us are actively searching for an intellectually honest and respectable faith, a faith that prizes scientific knowledge and literacy. From cutting-edge cosmology to genetics to evolutionary theory to particle physics to neuroscience, Christians want to investigate and enjoy the findings of science and integrate them with faith. But this pursuit, one I heartily approve of as a social scientist, can create tensions and raise hard and difficult questions: How does evolution fit with the book of Genesis? Or neuroscience with the belief in an immortal soul? The pursuit of a scientifically literate faith can move you deeper into doubt and increase the pressures of disenchantment. Many scientifically literate Christians find it hard to believe in ghosts, and this skepticism affects their beliefs in other supernatural beings—angels, demons, and the Devil. Even belief in God is affected. Across the board in this secular age, doubt haunts belief, which is why many believers are drifting toward agnosticism and atheism. The tide of disenchantment is simply too strong, and faith is swept away.

Consequently, a large part of being a scientifically engaged and literate Christian is swimming against this tide of doubt and disenchantment, and that's exhausting. Some days it seems like it would just be easier to stop struggling, to let the tide of disenchantment take you and drift into unbelief.

So why keep swimming?

Because the secular age isn't wholly characterized by disenchantment. Here and there in the secular, we encounter the transcendent, the holy, and the sacred. We encounter beauty and ugliness, love and meaning. We are skeptics, but we are also haunted by the sense that there is something more.

As Taylor describes it, the secular age is characterized by two cross-pressures. On the one hand is the downward pressure of skepticism and disenchantment, where the enchanted world is emptied out and all that is left is the flat, horizontal drama of human action and interaction. This is the trajectory of a *Scooby-Doo* episode, the journey to discover that, in the end, there are no ghosts or gods or devils. In the final analysis, at the end of the thirty-minute adventure, there are only human beings.

But here and there in this secular age we also experience updrafts of transcendence, a pull toward the heavens. We're interrupted by wonder and awe. We're surprised by joy. We experience a deep-seated ache and yearning, a feeling of restlessness, a longing for home. Even in an age of particle physics and brain scans, we still bump into the magic from time to time, still experience the enchantment of the world. We're skeptical and scientific people, yes, but we're also haunted by the suspicion that the universe is more than the sum of its subatomic parts.

Doubting and disenchanted Christians live at the center of these cross-pressures. We are skeptics, but we are also haunted in ways that agnostics or atheists are not. And that haunting keeps us swimming against the tide of disenchantment, keeps us tethered to faith through a restlessness and dissatisfaction with a thoroughly disenchanted world, a world ruled by the iron and deterministic laws of cause-and-effect.

Or Maybe We're Just Treading Water

But when you're swimming against the tide, you can't really make headway. You're simply holding your place, hanging on, working to keep yourself situated at the center of these cross-pressures. It's the only tenable place for the disenchanted Christian, this nexus of faith and doubt. Your alternatives are closing your mind to modern science—a scientific illiteracy far too many Christians adopt—or letting the disenchantment sweep you away toward atheism or agnosticism. In this secular age, faith and doubt will always go hand in hand, but it's hard work to hold your position at the center of these countervailing currents. Everything about faith is a struggle.

Given how intellectually, emotionally, and socially exhausting this effort is, doubting and disenchanted Christians resort to a variety of coping strategies. Here's one common technique: Believe as little as possible.

When belief is hard, one way to cope is to believe as little as possible. Believe only in what is absolutely necessary. Don't try to believe a lot of little, tangential things. Focus on the big stuff.

If belief is a big sack of rocks that you're carrying up the hill of faith, it makes sense to sort through the sack to examine each rock. Is this rock really necessary? If not, you can take that rock out of the sack to lighten your load.

Using this strategy, many of us have emptied the bag of faith down to a single rock, having jettisoned items of faith down to one single belief: *I believe in God.* Believing in God is the place where we focus all our time, energy, and attention. Only one rock to haul up the hill—belief in God—and not much else.

And let's say you're swimming with that bag of rocks, foolish as that may seem. When you're drowning, and beliefs are heavy weights, you drop as many weights as you can. And for many Christians, belief in God is the heaviest weight they can carry and still remain afloat.

So if you find it very hard simply to believe in God—if that is about the heaviest weight you can carry—then believing in, say, angels and demons is just too much to ask, especially in an age of science. It seems pretty obvious that demon possession in ancient times looks a lot like what we describe as mental illness. In addition, believing in demons doesn't seem all that essential to believing in God and following Jesus. And so, in the effort to keep faith simple, such beliefs are moved to the periphery of faith or jettisoned altogether.

But this creates problems. For one, we've got a Bible that is filled with references to angels and demons. We are told to "resist the Devil" (James 4:7), and Satan is described as our enemy, as a "lion prowling the earth seeking someone to devour" (1 Peter 5:8). In the Gospels, Jesus has conversations with both Satan (e.g., Matthew 4:1-11) and a legion of demons who had possessed a man (e.g., Luke 8:26-39). Given all our doubts and the pressures of disenchantment, what are going to do with all this spooky stuff in the Bible?

Scooby-Dooifying the Bible

Scooby-Doo is again helpful here.

In a *Scooby-Doo* episode, there's something sinister going on in the town, a real problem, a real source of wickedness. But the evil isn't spooky or supernatural as first suspected. The evil is moral, economic, and political in nature. The "demons" in *Scooby-Doo* are unmasked in the end to reveal the human face behind wickedness: It was Mr. Jenkins the crooked banker!

Disenchanted Christians do something similar when they encounter the Devil or demons in the Bible. Let's call this way of reading the Bible the *Scooby-Dooification* approach.

When reading a Bible story, we perform a Scooby-Dooification when we look past the spooky and supernatural covering to expose the human element at the core of the story. Just like in a *Scooby-Doo* episode. And what's important to keep in mind here is that

Scooby-Dooification isn't an attempt to "explain away" the story. As in the TV show, there's a real problem to be solved: Mr. Jenkins, the crooked banker, is actually robbing people. A Scooby-Dooification approach is simply looking for the Mr. Jenkins part of the story, where the seemingly spiritual problem is actually a human problem.

Scooby-Dooification, looking for the human element, is helpful for doubting Christians. Scooby-Dooification helps anchor us at the center of the cross-pressures of faith and disenchantment. Regarding the pressures of faith, Scooby-Dooification allows us to read a Bible story that contains a supernatural element in a way that recognizes a real problem in the world. The story isn't a fairy tale or a ghost story, we tell ourselves, because something *real* was happening. When we read that Jesus was "tempted of the Devil" we can, in good Scooby-Doo fashion, look past the supernatural aspect to appreciate the very real experience of *temptation*. And when we read that Jesus healed demon-possessed persons, we can debate whether Jesus was facing demons or mental illness.

Regardless, we can all agree that Jesus brought *real* relief to *real* people. With Scooby-Dooification we look for the human element to meet the demands of the modern, scientific worldview; then, to meet the demands of faith, we affirm that the story is true.

So the story is true, but in focusing on the human element the story becomes less heavy as an object of belief. Scooby-Dooification lightens the load for the doubting believers kicking hard against the tide of disenchantment. And to be clear, Scooby-Dooification isn't a denial of the supernatural element. There may be more— something supernatural—going on in the story. Maybe a whole lot more. We are back to the improv rule of *Yes, and*. A Scooby-Dooification reading of the story locates and affirms the human element. That's the *Yes*, the affirmation of truth. At a minimum, that much is going on the story. But that *Yes* can be followed up with an *and*. More can be added to the picture. Maybe something supernatural. Christians can debate what that *and* might look like. But a critical element in the story has been agreed on, the *Yes* to the human element in the story, with the rest held off to the side for a later discussion. All this helps lighten the load on the doubting Christian—fewer rocks to carry up the hill of faith.

Beyond lightening the load of doubts, Scooby-Dooification also reshapes how we describe spiritual warfare. Specifically, when we focus on the human element, our vision of spiritual warfare becomes more and more about social justice.

While that's easy to see in a *Scooby-Doo* episode, you might have a hard time seeing how this works when it comes to the Bible. For example, in a *Scooby-Doo* episode economic greed is usually the motivation behind the spooky activity going on in the town. The spooky covering is ripped away in the show to expose robbery, greed, economic exploitation, and political corruption. And if you read the Bible closely you see something similar going on in how it describes spiritual warfare. In the Bible, spiritual warfare is regularly tied up with political and economic exploitation. Just like a *Scooby-Doo* episode.

On Earth and in Heaven

To show how this Scooby-Dooification works, let's go to the bull's-eye for spiritual warfare talk in most churches. We all know the passage, quoted here from the King James Version:

> Put on the whole armour of God, that ye may be able to stand against the wiles of the devil. For we wrestle not against flesh and blood, but against principalities, against powers, against the rulers of the darkness of this world, against spiritual wickedness in high places. (Ephesians 6:11-12)

For many, this passage is the go-to text to show that Scooby-Dooification just isn't possible when it comes to spiritual warfare. Where Scooby-Dooification seeks to uncover the human element, Paul explicitly declares that our battle is *not* against "flesh and blood," that the battle is waged against "principalities and powers" and the "rulers of darkness." How much clearer can you get? When it comes to spiritual warfare, it seems that the door is closed on Scooby-Dooification.

But contrary to what it looks like, Ephesians 6:11-12 is actually one of the most important texts for Christians who look for the human element in biblical descriptions of spiritual warfare. Incredulous readers might ask: But how could that be if the text clearly says that our battle is *not* against flesh and blood?

The answer has to do with the Greek phrase in the text—*archai kai exousiai*—which is translated as "principalities and powers" and is used in the New Testament ten times. Interestingly and importantly, the only two occurrences of this phrase in the Gospels come in the Gospel of Luke and are references to human political institutions:

Luke 12:11
"When you are brought before synagogues, *rulers and authorities*, do not worry about how you will defend yourselves or what you will say . . ."

Luke 20:20
Keeping a close watch on him, they sent spies, who pretended to be honest. They hoped to catch Jesus in something he said so that they might hand him over to the *power and authority* of the governor.

When Jesus talks about conflict with "principalities and powers," he's talking about conflict with legal and political authorities. The Gospel describes conflict with "principalities and powers" as being arrested for disturbing the peace.

The other eight occurrences of *archai kai exousiai* in the New Testament occur in the Epistles. I'll list them all below and highlight the phrase as it appears in English translation. When you read each one, ask yourself this question: Are the powers being referred to in the passage human political powers, spiritual powers, or a mix of both?

1 Corinthians 15:24
Then the end will come, when he hands over the kingdom to
God the Father after he has destroyed all *dominion, authority*
and power.

Colossians 1:16
For by him all things were created: things in heaven and on
earth, visible and invisible, whether thrones or powers or *rulers
or authorities*; all things were created by him and for him.

Colossians 2:10
. . . and you have been given fullness in Christ, who is the head
over every *power and authority.*

Colossians 2:15
And having disarmed the *powers and authorities*, he made a
public spectacle of them, triumphing over them by the cross.

Ephesians 1:21
. . . far above all *rule and authority*, power and dominion, and
every title that can be given, not only in the present age but also
in the one to come.

Ephesians 3:10
His intent was that now, through the church, the manifold wisdom of God should be made known to the *rulers and authorities*
in the heavenly realms . . .

Ephesians 6:12
For our struggle is not against flesh and blood, but against the
rulers, against the *authorities*, against the powers of this dark
world and against the spiritual forces of evil in the heavenly
realms.

Titus 3:1
Remind the people to be subject to *rulers and authorities*, to be
obedient, to be ready to do whatever is good . . .

Are these human political powers, spiritual powers, or a mix of both? I expect that your answer was "a mix of both," with the exception of Titus 3:1, which, like the two instances in the Gospel of Luke, clearly points to human political powers. When Luke and Paul write about principalities and powers, they're talking about a mixture of human and spiritual powers.

The reason the Bible mixes and matches human and spiritual powers is because the writers of the Bible didn't think these were different sorts of powers. They are, instead, manifestations of the *same* power. In the ancient mind, spiritual and political powers were two sides of the same coin. Political power always had a divine aspect, for political and spiritual authority went hand in hand, each justifying and supporting the other. Kings were considered to be gods, demigods, or "sons of god." And the hierarchical ordering of ancient societies, with the king on top and slaves at the bottom, was believed to reflect a divine, heavenly order, which is why Ephesians 6 says that these political powers are in the "heavenly realm." When we think of Moses confronting Pharaoh with the demand, "Let my people go!," we tend to highlight the political struggle for justice, the emancipation of slaves from political and economic oppressors. But remember, Pharaoh wasn't a president or king. Pharaoh was a *god*, a divine being in the heavenly realm. In the Exodus, the *political* struggle on earth was also a *spiritual* struggle in the heavens. For the ancients, *justice* always had a *spiritual* aspect.

And while that might seem weird and superstitious, not much has changed. When we go to war, we fight for "God and Country." In this sense, all wars are "holy wars." In the Pledge of Allegiance we pledge to "one nation under God." We print "In God We Trust" on our money. And the most powerful people in our society are closer to the heavens, the "upper" class, high above the "middle" and "lower"-class folk. Political power and the spiritual power have always been tightly intertwined.

In sum, when Paul writes in Ephesians 6 that our battle is against the principalities and powers, he's not just talking about demon possession, he's also talking about our struggle with political powers. Focusing upon that political struggle allows for a Scooby-Doo–inspired reading of Ephesians 6, but with a focus less on human persons than human systems and institutions. Our spiritual struggle can focus on these unjust political and economic systems and the ideologies that justify their existence. Our battle is not against "flesh and blood"—individual human beings—but against *systemic* and *structural* evil. In the Bible, these systems are often identified with the image of Babylon, the violent and bloody symbol of empire in the Bible, the city that exploits the poor and weak. Spiritual warfare is resistance to empire, to the political and economic manifestations of Babylon in our own time and place. And with this vision in hand, the Scooby-Dooification of Ephesians 6 is complete. Spiritual warfare becomes social justice.

Yes, Social Justice, And . . .

This is where the conversation generally stops, with two different visions of spiritual warfare standing in opposition to one another. On the one hand is a vision found in many conservative churches where rebuking or binding Satan is common, along with petitions for a "hedge of angels," prayers requesting angelic protection for our churches, our families, our marriages or nation. On the other hand, many liberal and progressive Christians think about spiritual warfare as less concerned about angels and demons than about resisting the political and economic "principalities and powers" in the struggle for social justice. Two choices, pick one.

If you've tended to think of spiritual warfare as mainly about how our prayers give aid and strength to protective angels fighting off aggressive demons, I challenge you to expand how you think about spiritual warfare, because in the Bible spiritual conflict is intimately associated with political struggle. So I hope this insight leads you to explore a more politically and socially engaged vision of spiritual warfare.

But if you've already adopted this socially and politically engaged vision of spiritual warfare, I want you to expand your vision, too. For one thing, Jesus wasn't much of a political activist. When Jesus described the battle he was fighting, he talked more about Satan than about Caesar. And when spiritual warfare is reduced to political struggle it's tempted toward violence. For example, as we work for justice in the world, feelings can run hot; we're often tempted toward bitterness and hatred when we face the people we've identified as the cause of the problem. So if Jesus was an activist, he was an activist who preached "love your enemies" and "bless those who curse you." And that battle—the deep spiritual struggle to extend love, mercy, and grace for our enemies—must accompany any vision of Christian activism. Spiritual warfare isn't just political engagement, it's also a journey toward love.

A narrow focus on political activism also leaves out many pieces that in the Bible are critical to completing the puzzle. A narrow focus on political activism often ignores important conversations about personal morality and holiness. Political activism also tends to marginalize the church, the community Jesus left behind to continue his work. If electoral politics are how we are going to get things done in the world, going to church on Sunday to sing some worship songs seems pretty pointless. When spiritual warfare is reduced to social justice, things like church and morality get pushed to the side.

Basically, when you lose track of the Devil you lose track of Jesus and the kingdom of God.

Lastly, we don't often talk about this, but the fight for social justice exposes us to the pain and suffering of the world, and that exposure can take a heavy toll upon our faith. Compassion for the suffering of the world draws us deeper into the darkness of the world—a world of sex trafficking, rape, torture, genocide, child abuse, and starvation. And in the face of that massive and soul-crushing suffering a compassionate person has to ask: Why would a good, loving, and all-powerful God allow this? There's a sad irony here, how a compassionate faith places a heavy burden upon our faith. The greater our *compassion* for suffering, the greater our *doubts* as we face that suffering.

The deeper your compassion pulls you into the darkness, the heavier the burden your faith has to carry. Now we're adding rocks back into the sack.

You see the sad outcome, right? In the face of suffering, the greater the *compassion*, the greater the *doubt*. We want to build our faith upon a foundation of compassion, but that foundation can be unsteady and unsustainable if it lacks a supportive theology.

Many compassionate Christians are losing their faith because they lack this supportive theology, a theology that can reconcile their compassion with their doubts. And the heart and soul of that theology is what Greg Boyd calls a "theology of revolt."[2] In the face of doubts and disenchantment we need a vision of *spiritual resistance and struggle that energizes our faith in the face of pain and suffering.* To save our faith we must embrace spiritual warfare.

As paradoxical as it may seem, one of the reasons faith is harder for us is because we've given up talking about Old Scratch. Our faith has lost its fighting spirit. If we want to recover a vibrant and energized faith, we need to get over our awkwardness in talking about the Devil and spiritual warfare. Yes, social justice is a huge part of our battle to establish the kingdom of God on earth as it is in heaven. But there is more to spiritual warfare than social justice. Much more.

---

2. Gregory A. Boyd, *God at War: The Bible & Spiritual Conflict* (Downers Grove, IL: InterVarsity, 1997).

PART 2

To Destroy
the Devil's Work

*Spiritual Warfare
beyond Social Justice*

Chapter 3

Jesus the Exorcist

THOMAS JEFFERSON LOVED to cut up the Bible.

Thomas Jefferson—Founding Father, author of the Declaration of Independence, and the third President of the United States—was a Christian who didn't believe in the Devil or miracles. That makes Jefferson a lot like many Christians today. A man of the Enlightenment, and a man of science, Jefferson was one of the great apostles of the Age of Reason. And this thoroughly disenchanted Jefferson's Christianity. According to Jefferson, everything supernatural in the Bible could be dismissed as ancient backwardness and superstition. Jesus was the greatest moral teacher who ever lived, but Jesus wasn't a miracle worker. And when Jesus died, he didn't rise up from the dead.

But, sadly for Jefferson, the Gospels are chock-full of supernatural stuff. As a reasonable, scientifically literate Christian, what was Jefferson to do with a Jesus who raised the dead, healed the lepers, and cast out demons? Faced with this superstitious mess, Thomas Jefferson had an inspiring thought.

He reached for his scissors.

What's known as the *Jefferson Bible* is a version of the Gospels that was produced by Thomas Jefferson for his own personal edification. You can buy a copy on Amazon or in the gift shop at Monticello. And how Jefferson made his Bible was simplicity itself: using scissors and glue, Jefferson went through the Gospels and cut out every reference to the supernatural in Mark, Matthew, Luke, and John, and then he glued the pages back together.

Jesus healing the lepers? Snip. Calming the storm? Snip. Raising Lazarus? Snip. Casting out demons? Snip. Temptation in the wilderness? Snip.

The Resurrection? Snip.

Jefferson's snipping is the ultimate example of Scooby-Dooification. In snipping out all references to the supernatural, what Jefferson felt he had left in the Gospels was a simple historical and moral account of the life of Jesus of Nazareth. And while cutting up your Bible seems a bit extreme, we're not all that different from Thomas Jefferson. We might not use scissors, but when we get to references about the Devil in Bible, the words hardly register in our minds.

Snip.

If doubting and social justice–minded Christians love anything about Christianity, they love Jesus. For us Jesus is, quintessentially, the "friend of tax collectors and sinners" (Matthew 11:18), an example of love breaking down boundaries in welcoming the weak, oppressed, and marginalized. Jesus is the holy rebel facing down oppressive social, political, and religious institutions—the "principalities and powers" that eventually kill him.

And yet all this welcoming and rebelling in the New Testament is described in a curious way. Consider how Peter describes Jesus to Cornelius in Acts 10:

> You know what has happened throughout the province of Judea, beginning in Galilee after the baptism that John preached— how God anointed Jesus of Nazareth with the Holy Spirit and power, and how he went around doing good and healing all

who were under the power of the devil, because God was with him. (Acts 10:37-38)

Jesus went about doing good *and healing all who were under the power of the devil.* Christians who love the radical welcoming Jesus have emphasized the first part of this description—Jesus going around and doing good—but, in good Thomas Jefferson fashion, they've ignored the second part—Jesus overcoming the "power of the devil" in the lives of individuals. And yet, over and over in the New Testament, Jesus' witness and example—his good works—are consistently described *as spiritual warfare*, as a battle he was waging with Satan. 1 John 3:8 sums it up this way: "The reason the Son of God appeared was to destroy the devil's work."

So let's get biblical about it: if Jesus was anything, he was an exorcist. This is especially highlighted in the earliest Gospel, Mark, which starts with a bang. There's no genealogy or nativity scene. Instead, Mark begins with John the Baptist, and Jesus is baptized by the time we get to the eleventh verse. Satan shows up a couple of verses later, tempting Jesus at the start of his public ministry, inaugurating a conflict that we can trace through the all stories to come. In verses 14 and 15 Jesus proclaims the good news—"The kingdom of God has come!"—and in verses 16 through 18 he calls his first followers. Less than twenty verses into Mark and the stage has been set.

Jesus then begins his ministry with an exorcism. In verse 21 we read of Jesus healing a man with an unclean spirit. The people are amazed at this display of spiritual authority, declaring: "What is this? A new teaching—and with authority! He even gives orders to impure spirits and they obey him." Word spreads about this exorcist and the people descend upon him:

> That evening after sunset the people brought to Jesus all the sick and demon-possessed. The whole town gathered at the door, and Jesus healed many who had various diseases. He also drove out many demons, but he would not let the demons speak because they knew who he was. (Mark 1:32-34)

Up all night exorcising demons and surely exhausted, Jesus goes off by himself to pray early in the morning, eventually deciding to move on to confront "the power of the devil" in other towns:

> Jesus replied, "Let us go somewhere else—to the nearby villages—so I can preach there also. That is why I have come." So he traveled throughout Galilee, preaching in their synagogues and driving out demons. (Mark 1:38-39)

Jesus moves throughout Galilee driving out demons and preaching about the kingdom. Exorcism was at the heart of Jesus' ministry and the focal demonstration of his kingdom proclamation. That people were being set free from the power of the devil was the sign that God's kingdom had been inaugurated in the person of Jesus. The kingdom of God and exorcism go hand-in-hand.

It should not surprise us, then, after reading the first chapter of Mark, that in Acts Peter describes the ministry of Jesus as going from place to place "doing good" and "healing all those under the power of the devil." That's exactly what we see Jesus doing throughout all four of the Gospels: doing good and confronting Satan. And that's the ministry that the apostles continue in the book of Acts, the ministry of exorcism.

We can trace this confrontation between Jesus and Satan as the grand dramatic plotline of the Gospel accounts, and of the entire Bible. The seeds of the conflict are sown right at the very start in the book of Genesis when Satan successfully deceives Adam and Eve, enslaving the world to sin and death. With the world now in bondage to these dark powers, Satan becomes "the ruler of the world"— a hungry predator roaming the face of the earth looking for people to devour.

Finding us weak and vulnerable to Satan's attacks, Jesus is born into the world to "destroy the work of the devil," to set us free from Satan's reign of terror. As the Gospels tell the story, when Jesus is born into the world a power struggle ensues. Satan tries to kill Jesus as an infant, and it's only due to angelic intervention that the child escapes. Later, after God publicly identifies Jesus as the Messiah at his baptism, Satan moves to defeat Jesus in a direct confrontation, tempting Jesus in the wilderness. Satan fails but is determined to "wait for an opportune time" to attack again. Like Arnold Schwarzenegger in *The Terminator*, Old Scratch will be back.

For the next three years Satan and Jesus confront each other in the lives of suffering people as Jesus goes from town to town doing good and healing all who were under the power of the Devil. By driving out the Prince of this World Jesus declares that the kingdom of God has been inaugurated on earth. And as the kingdom expands, Jesus' followers report that they too have power over Satan! Hearing this, Jesus sees Satan falling like lightning from heaven. Victory is at hand.

But Old Scratch, he's not going to go down so easily. On the brink of defeat, Satan enters the heart of Judas, setting up Jesus' betrayal, arrest, and crucifixion. On Good Friday the battle was over. Old Scratch had won. Jesus was dead.

But on Easter Sunday Jesus was resurrected from the dead, decisively defeating all the dark forces arrayed against him, us, and the entire creation. Sin, death, and the Devil were all defeated. The gates of Hades did not prevail. The kingdom of God has been inaugurated upon the earth and Jesus has ascended to the right hand of the Father. Jesus now rules as Lord of all. And the reign of King Jesus continues to expand until he has defeated all dominion, power, and authority on earth. And the final powers to be defeated? Death and Old Scratch himself, pitched into the Lake of Fire at the dawn of the New Heavens and the New Earth.

Don't Snip the Devil out of the Story

We don't often tell the story of the Gospels in this way, with Jesus battling the Satan for control over the earth. Most of this story is mentally cut out, excised and left as scraps on Thomas Jefferson's floor. We prefer to see Jesus as a moral teacher, especially when he calls out corrupt religious, political, and economic institutions. But if you excise the dramatic clash between Jesus and the Devil you eliminate the narrative glue that holds the Gospels together as a coherent story. If we want to understand what Jesus was up to in the world, we've got to confront his conflict with Satan and acknowledge how central that plotline is to the story being told in the Gospels.

All this presents a problem for Christians who, like Thomas Jefferson, mentally snip the Devil out of the Gospels. Jesus sits at the heart of Christianity, but the majority of Christians appear to doubt the central dramatic element of Jesus' ministry and the central sign of Jesus' kingdom proclamation: his confrontation and the defeat of Satan in this world. We place Jesus at the center, but the Jesus we place there has been radically separated from his central, defining work. A Jesus who isn't engaged in conflict with Satan isn't the Jesus of the Gospels. The reason the Son of God appeared was to destroy the Devil's work.

The implication here should be clear: If we want to fight the battle Jesus was fighting in the world, we have to understand the nature of that battle. In his book *Simply Jesus*, N. T. Wright describes the situation well:

> Wherever we look, it appears that Jesus was aware of a great battle in which he was already involved and that would, before too long, reach some kind of climax.
>
> This was not, it seems, the battle that his contemporaries, including his own followers, expected him to fight. It wasn't even the same sort of battle—though Jesus used the language of battle to describe it. Indeed, as the Sermon on the Mount seems to indicate, fighting itself, in the normal physical sense, was precisely what he was not going to do. There was a different kind of battle in the offing, a battle that had already begun. In this battle, it was by no means as clear as those around Jesus would have liked as to who was on which side, or indeed whether "sides" was the right way to look at things. The battle

in question was a different sort of thing, because it had a different sort of enemy. . . .The battle Jesus was fighting was against the satan.[1]

Jesus was in a battle with Satan, and if we want to follow Jesus we have to fight the battle that Jesus fought. This seems a rather obvious point, but with all the mental snipping going on, due to our doubts and disenchantment, this point is often missed. Jesus was picking a fight. Followers of Jesus have to pick that same fight.

Too many Christians are playing Thomas Jefferson with Jesus. We wind up following a Swiss Cheese Jesus, a Jesus full of holes, snipped to suit our preferences and prejudices. And when it comes to Jesus' battle with Satan, both conservative and progressive Christians snip out critical parts of the conflict.

With their focus on traditional family values, the Protestant work ethic, and "God and Country" patriotism, conservative Christians snip out the Jesus who marginalized the family, who was a friend of sinners, who sided with the poor against the rich, and who was executed by the state for sedition. Snip. Snip. Snip.

Progressive Christians snip out different stuff. We're aware that Jesus was executed by the state but fail notice that Jesus' battle with the Satan didn't look a whole lot like what we'd describe as political activism. Jesus lived under empire, one of the most exploitative and oppressive in world history. And yet, Jesus never led a protest against Roman occupation. Jesus didn't lead a "March on Rome" or carry a sign through downtown Jerusalem protesting Roman oppression. Jesus' one disruptive action, clearing the Temple, was the restoration of a house of worship so that it could be a house of prayer. And most worryingly, Jesus was routinely gracious to the colonial occupiers and agents of empire like tax collectors and Roman centurions, to say nothing of telling his oppressed countrymen to "love your enemies."

---

1. N. T. Wright, *Simply Jesus: Who He Was, What He Did, Why It Matters* (New York: HarperOne, 2011), 119–20.

We've failed to grasp the exact *nature* of Jesus' provocation because of all the snipping that's been going on. With Old Scratch snipped out of the Gospels, we've lost track of what Jesus was up to and why he was killed.

The War to End All Wars

If we want to avoid Swiss Cheese Jesus we have to grasp how Jesus' kingdom proclamation was deeply political *and* deeply spiritual. In proclaiming the good news that the kingdom of God was at hand, Jesus was calling Israel back to her vocation to be a blessing to the nations by inviting us into the gracious reign of God on earth. Progressive Christians frequently miss this point, but Jesus called *Israel* to repentance, not Rome. God was and is blessing the world through the establishment of a kingdom on earth, a kingdom Christians believe was inaugurated in the life and ministry of Jesus. And this kingdom was and is established over against the empires of the world. But Jesus' conflict with Rome—and the empire of any age— wasn't a direct political confrontation but involved the establishment a kingdom that was and is *a rival location of human flourishing* that affects every aspect of life—spiritual, moral, social, and even political. Jesus' conflict with the Satan was the struggle to establish God's rule across all these intersecting spheres, the ways in which political oppression is wrapped up in spiritual and moral bondage. This is why Jesus' message of liberation was connected to his ministry of exorcism, why Jesus was "doing good" *and* releasing people from "the power of the devil." The battle for the kingdom is fought on multiple fronts, but the enemy is the same.

I've only recently come to comprehend all this, the political and spiritual intersections of the kingdom. It's a lesson I learned talking about Old Scratch out at the prison.

I was drawn to prison work because of my concerns about social justice—I'm concerned about mass incarceration, the New Jim Crow, capital punishment, and the injustices and inhumanity of our criminal justice system. But the inmates out at the prison, the Men in

White I've come to care so much about, are struggling with so much more than political injustice. They struggle with their own inner darkness and demons. They struggle to hold on to faith, hope, and love. They long for redemption and forgiveness. The men thirst for a touch of kindness, gentleness, and humanity. Politically, I care enormously about the injustices of our prison system in the U.S., and I'm politically engaged on the frontlines of that battle. But on the spiritual front, prisons are very dark places. So while I want to do good like Jesus and fight the political battles, I also want to enter into the darkness to heal all those under power of devil. I want to be an exorcist.

And the Men in White are my exorcists. Just this week, after I shared some of my struggles, the Men in White gathered around to lay hands on me and pray, "Lord, protect Richard from Evil One, protect him from Old Scratch." Amen to that.

For my birthday this year, the Men in White gave me a prison-made birthday card. All the guys had signed it. It's quite an impressive piece of artwork. The card has shiny foil intricately embedded in the edges making it sparkle, foil scavenged from the tops of yogurt cups and the glue cooked up from some old prison recipe.

Inside the card was a folded piece of paper, a poem one of the inmates had written for me. Here is a bit of it:

> I can't count how many times
> you've lightened the mood
> and lifted my spirit.
> You never judge,
> which is the most amazing thing.
> That takes a huge amount of generosity
> and wisdom on your part.
> No wonder I find it so easy
> to relax around you, to say
> what I really think, to just be myself.
> Thank you for another year.

Healing those under the power of the devil. I don't know exactly what it means to be an exorcist. But I think it looks a little bit like that.

Chapter 4

The White Witch

RECENTLY I SPENT a week with some U.S. missionaries from my faith tradition who are working in European counties. They've got a difficult job. Compared to the United States, Europe is very secularized, which makes it hard on missionaries wanting to proclaim the "good news" in these contexts.

And what makes it particularly difficult in secularized contexts is that before these missionaries can get to the good news, because of the way they think about Jesus' death on the cross, they have to convince an unbelieving and secular audience about the "bad news."

Here's the good news. The good news is that Jesus died to save you from your sins and eternal punishment, which is great news—but there's a problem. The bad news is that you are a sinner bound for eternal damnation.

So you can see the predicament the missionaries are facing: before they can talk about Jesus, they have to convince you that you have this really, really big problem: you are sinner, heading to hell.

That's not a very cheery message. Given the secular context in which these missionaries are working, they have to spend most of their time convincing people of the bad news before they can turn to the good news. Which makes the *bad* news the *first* news anyone is hearing about Christianity.

This presentation of the gospel is a simple two-step process:

Step 1: First, The Bad News

You are a sinner bound for hell.

Step 2: Next, The Good News

But Jesus died to save you!

You can't get to Step 2 (*Jesus!*) until you convince people of Step 1 (*Damnation!*). But how do you convince people who don't even believe in God that they are sinners condemned to hell by God? It's a tough sell.

We're headed in the same direction in the U.S. As the rate of the religiously unaffiliated grows, along with rates of atheism and agnosticism, America is looking increasingly like Europe, which means that American Christians are also increasingly flummoxed with how best to proclaim the good news to a culture that barely believes in God, let alone a God who is damning them to hell.

But the problems here actually run a bit deeper, problems that give even Christians a whole a lot of heartburn. And when your message isn't selling well with the home team, well, your sales pitch is really going to struggle on the road.

The heartburn has to do with common conceptions about how Jesus' death upon the cross functioned as a sacrifice to bring about reconciliation between God and humanity. The most common version of atonement in Protestant and evangelical churches is a view called *penal substitutionary atonement*. You likely know the basic idea: Our sin brings us under the judgment of a holy and just God; we deserve death and eternal punishment for our sins, but because God loves us God provides a means for our salvation; on the cross Jesus takes our place, substituting himself for us, taking upon himself our sin and enduring the just punishment of our sin. Jesus' death is a sacrifice that atones for our sin by appeasing the wrath and judgment of God. And by accepting Jesus as my savior I stand forgiven and holy in the eyes of God.

Jesus' death, then, is the solution to our problem, the fact that we are, in the words of Jonathan Edwards's famous sermon, "Sinners in the hands of an angry God." Consequently, to understand how Jesus' death on the cross is good news for us we have to be convinced that his death is an atoning and substituting sacrifice for us, which means we have to be convinced that such a sacrifice was necessary in the first place. We have to believe that we are sinners in the hands of an angry God.

To be sure, penal substitutionary atonement is good news for anyone convinced that, because of their sin, they deserve the wrath and judgment of God. But there are also a lot of worries about the view of God that sits behind penal substitutionary atonement.

There are two related worries. The first worry has to do with why those missionaries felt they had to start with the bad news. Specifically, for penal substitutionary atonement to work, *God* has to be your problem. In penal substitutionary atonement, Jesus is saving you from the wrath of God. Some might counter that *sin* is the real problem, the way our sin brings us under God's judgment. Fair point, but God could choose to be more forgiving, merciful, loving, and tolerant of human sin. Since God created us God should understand that we're *human*, mistake-prone and fallible creatures. Moral perfection isn't a reasonable expectation. So why does God get so angry? So angry to want to kill us or torment us in hell for all eternity?

Plus, when you look on the loving, forgiving, and nonviolent Jesus—Jesus the friend of sinners—the sinners-in-the-hands-of-an-angry-God view of the atonement just doesn't make a lot of sense. In contrast to Jesus—the Jesus who is the "exact representation" of God (Hebrews 1:3)—the God of penal substitutionary atonement seems violently intolerant of sin. These two visions of God just don't fit together. Can't and won't fit together. Something is wrong.

The other worry about penal substitutionary atonement is how blood functions in this system. Specifically, God demands a blood sacrifice in order to be appeased. And given the history of violence in

Christianity—from the Crusades to the Inquisition—a bloodthirsty God is very worrisome.

Again, the contrast here with Jesus is perplexing. Jesus was decidedly nonviolent, willing to shed *his own blood* rather than the blood of others. Consequently, it is very hard, if not impossible, to reconcile the nonviolence of Jesus—who is the "exact representation" of God—with the violent and bloodthirsty God of penal substitutionary atonement.

So much heartburn is caused by all these questions that many are rejecting penal substitutionary atonement as both a *false* and *dangerous* theory about what happened to Jesus on the cross. Far too many have seen or experienced the terror created by the God lurking behind penal substitutionary atonement, to say nothing of the guilt and shame associated with the notion that God finds you loathsome to the point of desiring your death and eternal torment. The psychological damage that the theory of penal substitutionary atonement has caused has been enormous, causing many to flee the faith.

But if we reject penal substitutionary atonement, then something has to take its place. Some answer has to be given about why Jesus died upon the cross and why his death brings about our salvation.

An Atonement in Which God Is Not the Problem

If we want the death of Jesus on the cross to be truly good news, two things have to happen. First, the good news of Jesus' death actually has to be *good* news. Not bad news first and good news second. Just 100 percent, undiluted good news. Second, the good news of Jesus' death has to replace the vision of Jonathan Edwards's "angry God." Jesus' death must be the demonstration of a loving, nonviolent God. As the "exact representation" of God, Jesus and God have to be on the same page. God always has to look and behave like Jesus. And that rules out a bloodthirsty God who demands the death of sinners as the payment of sin.

As it turns out, there are actually quite a few theories of Jesus' death that meet these demands, but one that has gotten a lot of attention is a view that also has the benefit of being the first and earliest understanding of the atonement. This view is called Christus Victor—that's Latin for Christ the Victor.

For the first 1,000 years of the church, Christus Victor was the dominant understanding of what happened on the cross. And this mix—an atonement theory with an ancient pedigree that addresses modern concerns—has made Christus Victor one of the more popular alternatives to penal substitutionary atonement.

According to Christus Victor, humanity and the entire created order is in oppressive bondage to a variety of cosmic forces, including sin and death, forces the Devil uses to keep us separated from God. In response to our bondage to these powers, Jesus is born into the world to liberate us and set us free. Jesus rescues us from enslavement to hostile spiritual forces rather than from the wrath and judgment of God.

One difference between Christus Victor atonement and penal substitutionary atonement is illustrated in how the death of Christ functions in a very old example of Christus Victor theology, what is called the "ransom theory" of the atonement. For example, in the New Testament the death of Jesus is occasionally described as a "ransom" payment. As the Gospel of Mark declares, Jesus came to give his life "as a ransom for many" (Mark 10:45). And a ransom assumes that humanity is being held hostage.

It doesn't make much sense to think God is holding us hostage. So the early Christians believed that it was Satan who was holding humanity hostage and demanding a ransom. In order to free us, then, Jesus exchanges his life for ours, pays the ransom, and sets us free from the power of the Devil.

This idea might seem pretty strange, but you've likely encountered it before, as this is the same atonement theory on display in C. S. Lewis's *The Lion, the Witch and the Wardrobe.* You recall the story. Edmund betrays his family to the White Witch, the Satan figure of Narnia. Because of his betrayal Edmund belongs to the Witch. In her confrontation with Aslan, who is the rightful ruler of Narnia, the White Witch says of Edmund, "That human creature is mine. His life is forfeit to me. His blood is my property."

In order to set Edmund free from the claim and power of the White Witch, Aslan exchanges his life for Edmund's. The White Witch accepts the ransom, and Edmund is set free.

But as we know, the story doesn't end there. Aslan is killed, paying the price of Edmund's sin, suffering his death penalty. And by killing Aslan the White Witch thinks she has won a great victory, that her ultimate foe has been vanquished. But Aslan is raised back to life, cracking the Stone Table, the source of the White Witch's cultic power, and rolling back death itself.

The whole dynamic dramatized by *The Lion, the Witch and the Wardrobe* is described quite succinctly in the book of Hebrews:

> Since the children have flesh and blood, he too shared in their humanity so that by his death he might break the power of him who holds the power of death—that is, the devil—and free those who all their lives were held in slavery by their fear of death. (Hebrews 2:14-15)

That's Christus Victor atonement, Jesus setting us free from the Devil and the power of death. Just like Aslan sets Edmund free from the White Witch and cracks the Stone Table in *The Lion, the Witch and the Wardrobe*.

Recall the worry about the view of God sitting behind penal substitutionary atonement, that we are sinners in the hands of an angry God. Notice how things are changed in *The Lion, the Witch and the Wardrobe*. Aslan isn't saving Edmund from the wrath of God. Aslan saves Edmund *from the White Witch*—she's the problem, the enemy to be defeated. In Christus Victor, *God* isn't your problem. Your problem is *an enslavement to oppressive spiritual forces*. Consequently, God's actions in the story—like Aslan's actions in *The Lion, the Witch and the Wardrobe*—are wholly loving and benevolent. When Aslan gives his life as a ransom for Edmund, there is no vengeance, no wrath, no hell, and no damnation. There is only self-giving love. It's the Witch who is bloodthirsty and demanding a sacrifice. Aslan is wholly nonviolent. The bloodlust is all on the side of the Witch.

But Who Exactly Is Christ Victorious Over?

With its vision of a wholly loving and nonviolent God, Christus Victor is an attractive alternative to penal substitutionary atonement. Perhaps, if this is your first exposure to Christus Victor, you've become attracted to the view. I mean, who doesn't like Aslan saving Edmund? And yet, despite its recent surge in popularity there are some things about Christus Victor theology that haven't been given enough attention, especially among doubting and disenchanted Christians.

The Devil plays a big role in Christus Victor atonement. But if the majority of Christians don't believe in the Devil, it's hard to see how Christus Victor atonement can work for doubting and disenchanted believers. The Devil is a key part of the Christus Victor package. Christus Victor atonement doesn't work if there isn't a White Witch.

Of course, for Christians who do believe in the Devil, there's neither doubt nor disenchantment to interfere with exploring Christus Victor as an alternative to penal substitutionary atonement. However, if you're attracted to Christus Victor but don't believe in the Devil, or at least have significant doubts, you've got some work to do. Christus Victor requires a theology of spiritual warfare, a vision of spiritual enslavement. We're drawn to the loving and nonviolent God in Christus Victor atonement but we fail to appreciate the "warfare worldview" the view assumes, that there's conflict between God and Satan, between Aslan and the White Witch.[1]

---

1. The phrase "warfare worldview" comes from Greg Boyd. See Gregory A. Boyd, *God at War: The Bible & Spiritual Conflict* (Downers Grove, IL: InterVarsity, 1997).

Christus Victor theology doesn't require a belief in a literal, personal Devil, but at minimum you have to believe that humans are enslaved or trapped by oppressive spiritual forces, because the core idea of Christus Victor atonement is the belief that God is acting in Jesus as a liberator, emancipator, and rescuer. And if God in Jesus is engaged in a Great Rescue Operation, we have to assume *a prior condition* in which we experienced spiritual slavery and oppression. To revisit 1 John 3:8, "the reason the Son of God appeared was to destroy the devil's work." And if that's the case, we need to be able to describe "the devil's work" and exactly how Jesus destroyed it.

One way to describe "the devil's work" is to resort again to Scooby-Dooification, to look for the human and political element in any talk about slavery and emancipation. We don't need to talk about *spiritual* liberation, some say, when there's enough work to do with *political* liberation. We can think about Christus Victor in concrete political terms. Instead of talking about slavery to the Devil we can talk about *physical* bondage, like the slaves in global sex trafficking, or *economic* bondage, like wage slavery.

I most definitely think we can and must think about liberation in concrete political terms, but if we restrict our vision to the political realm we're going to miss some rather obvious things. Again, when we lose track of the Devil we lose track of the heart of the struggle. For example, you might do good work freeing young girls from the hands of sex traffickers, but will that stop global sex trafficking in the world? Why does sex trafficking exist in the first place? Where's that darkness coming from? Focusing on concrete political work tends to leave these larger questions unaddressed; it fails to attend to the diabolical element at work in the background, a background where the moral, political, and spiritual elements are all mixed up together. Fighting evil in the world is like Hercules fighting the Hydra: cut off one head and two come back in its place. Political oppression doesn't just drop out of the sky. To think you can talk about the Holocaust or human sex trafficking and avoid a conversation about sin and wickedness is naïve. And dangerous. You have to attend to the spiritual darkness at work in the background. And the potency of Christus Victor is that it *assumes this diabolical backdrop*, envisioning salvation as liberation from what Paul describes as "the present evil age" (Galatians 1:4) and from "spiritual forces of wickedness" (Ephesians 6:12).

So let us not be deceived. The White Witch is still at work. The Devil is real and much of the world remains in spiritual bondage.

And so the battle is joined. We enter the darkness as children of the kingdom to give witness to the resurrection. The power of the Devil has been defeated. The ransom was paid. The Stone Table has been cracked. The power of death is being rolled back.

The White Witch is on the run. And Aslan is on the move.

Chapter 5

Holy Ghost
Conga Lines

I LEARNED TO talk about the Devil at a place where we dance in a Holy Ghost conga line.

My church in Abilene, Texas—the Highland Church of Christ—has an outreach named Freedom Fellowship. Freedom's building is on the south side of town in an economically depressed neighborhood. At Freedom we welcome the poor and homeless, to those struggling with addictions, and to men and women paroled from prison who are working to reintegrate back into society. If you visit Freedom you'll find us smoking on the steps, wearing ankle monitors, attending Twelve Step meetings, sleeping at the Salvation Army, or living in halfway houses.

And you'll also find us eating and worshiping together.

Every Wednesday night at Freedom we serve a meal that's followed by a worship service. Some of our neighbors who join us for dinner don't stay for worship, and that's perfectly okay. But most of us do stay. After dinner Michael and the praise band start up, and with the start of the music, hands start to rise. David, always in the front row, starts beating out an insistent (and slightly off-beat) *ching-ching-ching* on his dove-shaped tambourine. The congregation starts to sway. Some grab pieces of fabric from a basket to wave as praise veils. Some dance in the aisles. And throughout the evening, exclamations of "Thank you, Jesus!" and "Amen!" and "Come on now!" punctuate our worship, readings, and preaching.

I've been living and worshiping with the Freedom community for about as long as I've been leading the Bible study out at the prison. Freedom is the community where I'm learning lessons about friendships that give and receive across the racial, educational, and socioeconomic lines that divide so much of American society. Because I'm an educator, I'm often tapped to preach and teach at Freedom, but I prefer to help each week with transportation (a lot of our members don't have cars) and cleaning up after our meals, washing the dishes or mopping the floor.

It's no exaggeration when I say that Freedom saved my faith—Freedom and the prison Bible study. Years ago when I first started coming to Freedom my faith was jaded, skeptical, cynical, overeducated, and elitist. And being a college professor, it didn't help that I spent most of my time with other Christians who were jaded, skeptical, cynical, overeducated, and elitist. My faith had become very dry, almost nonexistent. My faith had become *philosophy*, a collection of ideas to kick around with other smart people in a coffeeshop or pub. The notion that anyone could be *enthusiastic* about faith, that faith could be passionate and vital, was foreign to me, akin to talking about Martians—Christians from a strange and alien planet. To be a passionate and enthusiastic Christian was to be naïve and unsophisticated, one of those hand-raising, dancing in the aisles, holy roller types.

So you can imagine just how awkward and out of place I felt when I first started going to Freedom. Talk about a fish out of water. I was a jaded and overeducated PhD sitting smack in the middle of a Pentecostal tent revival.

I use the word *enthusiastic* deliberately, for it comes from the Greek root *entheos* (literally *en* "in" + *theos* "God"), meaning to be filled by God. An *enthusiastic* Christian is a Christian *who has been filled by God*. And in a word, that's what I encountered at Freedom: *enthusiastic* Spirit-filled believers—an enthusiastic, Spirit-filled experience that I keenly knew I lacked.

Both the Men in White and the saints at Freedom describe God in very immanent terms. We speak of God's Spirit as being ever present and ever at work in the details and minutiae of our lives. A synonym for immanent is *indwelling*. And that's exactly how we experience God—the Holy Spirit indwelling every aspect of life.

In a word, the spirituality you encounter at Freedom and the prison is *enchanted*, the very opposite of the disenchanted spirituality that characterized my faith, a dry, overintellectualized faith that marginalized emotion and experience to focus on ideas, reading lots of books and throwing around theological terms like "eschatological" and "soteriological." At Freedom and with the Men in White, God's Spirit fills and enchants the world. In the words of the Catholic poet Gerard Manley Hopkins, we see that "the world is charged with the grandeur of God." Or in the words of the psalmist,

Where can I go from your Spirit?
Where can I flee from your presence?
If I go up to the heavens, you are there;
if I make my bed in the depths, you are there.
If I rise on the wings of the dawn,
if I settle on the far side of the sea,
even there your hand will guide me,
your right hand will hold me fast.
If I say, "Surely the darkness will hide me
and the light become night around me,"
even the darkness will not be dark to you;
the night will shine like the day,
for darkness is as light to you. (Psalm 139:7-12)

The world is enchanted, filled with the Spirit, filled with the grandeur of God, a Presence that, no matter where we go, we cannot escape.

Re-Enchanting Christianity

If we had to attach adjectives to this enchanted spirituality, the best might be *charismatic* or *pentecostal* (small *p*), and what I discovered is that my experience with the charismatic faith of Freedom wasn't unique. As sociologists of religion will tell you, charismatic Christianity has always been the spirituality of the persecuted and the oppressed— enchanted, charismatic spirituality is the Christianity of the margins. While the Christian faith is on the decline in secular, disenchanted America and Europe, it's exploding in Africa and Latin America, especially among the poor. And the Christianity that is growing and thriving far away from the centers of geopolitical power is distinctively charismatic and pentecostal. As the worldwide Christian population becomes ethnically darker and poorer—as Christianity's center of gravity shifts away from rich, white America toward the poor in Africa and Latin America—it's also becoming more enchanted.

All this places white, rich, educated Western Christianity in a very awkward spot, the same awkwardness I experienced when I first worshiped at Freedom. Once during my early days at Freedom a sort of Holy Ghost conga line broke out as worshipers formed a line, hands on the shoulders in front of them, and danced around the sanctuary. It threw me for a loop. Feeling awkward, I elected to stay in my seat and give people high fives as they passed me—it seemed like the encouraging thing to do.

At Freedom we lay hands on each other in prayer. We anoint with oil. We wave praise veils. We pray to cast out demons. We share personal testimonies of God's work among us. We experience the presence and guidance of the Holy Spirit.

At Freedom *we expect miracles.*

And it's the same out at the prison: "Lord, protect us from Old Scratch!"

As a disenchanted and doubting Christian who would raise a skeptical eyebrow at any spooky tale about demon possession or guardian angels, I didn't know what to do with the charismatic, enchanted spirituality of Freedom and the prison. And that's the irony. What brought me to these places in the first place was that I cared about social justice and oppression.

When I first went out to the prison, the head chaplain asked me why I wanted to volunteer. I replied, "Matthew 25. The Parable of the Sheep and the Goats. Jesus said 'I was in prison and you visited me.' So I'm out here to do that." This is the same reason why I started attending Freedom. Matthew 25. Feed the hungry, clothe the naked, house the homeless. That's what Freedom does. That's why I'm there.

It was my passion for social justice that drew me to Freedom and the prison. To the incarcerated. To the homeless. To the poor and hungry. But my passion for social justice was flowing out of a disenchanted, politicized vision of "spiritual warfare." I was drawn to these places because of Scooby-Dooification. Spiritual warfare wasn't about spooky demons or angels, it was about social justice, battling the principalities and powers at work in systemic oppression that sent me out to the prison and got me mopping the floors at Freedom.

But here's the irony: A disenchanted, politicized, and progressive vision of spiritual warfare drew me to the margins and there, once I found myself on the margins, I clashed with the enchanted, enthusiastic, and charismatic spirituality I encountered.

There I was, a doubting believer, faith hanging by an intellectual string, giving out high fives to a Holy Ghost conga line.

World(view)s Colliding

When your Christianity is enchanted, you talk a lot about the Devil. At least that's been my experience. The charismatic spirituality at Freedom and out at the prison assumes a "warfare worldview" where the spiritual forces of light are waging war against the forces of darkness. So when doubting and disenchanted Christians stand with the oppressed, worlds will collide—one disenchanted, the other enchanted—and we've got to figure out what to do about this collision.

It might seem that there are no good options here. One the one hand, it seems like a waste of time to try to convince disenchanted Western Christians to start believing in Old Scratch, because you can't force beliefs. On the other hand, I don't want to talk about the Devil at Freedom or the prison in a way that is elitist and paternalistic. I don't approach requests for deliverance with a wink and knowing smile. I don't want to talk about the Devil ironically. I don't want to pray "Lord, protect us from Old Scratch" with my fingers crossed.

So I'm left looking for middle ground. I want to embrace and learn from the charismatic spirituality I've encountered at Freedom and in the prison, but I don't feel that I can give up the hard and critical investigations that have shaped and enriched my faith but given it a skeptical edge.

I propose three ideas to guide this ship between Scylla and Charybdis.

First, to the point of this book, doubting and disenchanted Christians must expand our vision of spiritual warfare to include more than social justice. There is a uniquely moral and spiritual component to spiritual warfare. While doubts may linger about the existence of disembodied spirits, we can talk about spiritual warfare—and even angels and demons—in ways that have integrity and authenticity. So let's start learning how to talk again about Old Scratch.

Second, we have to embrace the fact that God's "preferential option" for the poor and suffering—as the liberation theologians like to put it—is as *theological* as it is political and economic. I like the way Howard Thurman describes the "preferential option" in his book *Jesus and the Disinherited*, a book it is said that Martin Luther King Jr. carried with him wherever he went. Christianity is only good news, Thurman writes, if it's good news for "those who stand, at a moment in human history, with their backs against the wall."[1] God's preferential option is solidary and support for those with their backs against the wall. And this includes *theological* solidarity,[2] embracing, supporting, and standing with the enchanted, charismatic spirituality that *is experienced as good news* among those whose backs are against the wall.

Finally, while theological solidary might not dispel our doubts and disenchantment, it will open us to enchantment. In his book about pentecostal spirituality, *Thinking in Tongues*, James Smith says that the enchantment of charismatic spirituality flows out of a radical openness to God.[3] In the words of C. S. Lewis, this openness is a willingness to be "surprised by Joy."[4] At root, enchantment is simply a holy openness to Divine surprise. Enchantment isn't forcing yourself to believe in unbelievable things, it's allowing yourself to be interrupted and surprised by God.

This posture of radical openness to Divine surprise is how I approach my life at Freedom. I've worked hard to use the language of spiritual warfare in a way that is authentic, and I marginalize my doubts to embrace the good news as it's experienced by my friends who live with their backs against the wall.

But most importantly, I simply open myself up to enchantment.

Whenever I walk past the barbed wire to enter the prison or begin to hear the *ching-ching-ching* of David's dove-shaped tambourine, I turn outward with a sense of expectation.

I open my heart and mind so that I can be surprised anew by the joy of the Holy Ghost conga line.

---

1. Howard Thurman, *Jesus and the Disinherited* (Boston, MA: Beacon, 1996), 11.

2. I owe this insight to my friend Brad East.

3. James K. A. Smith, *Thinking in Tongues: Pentecostal Contributions to Christian Philosophy* (Grand Rapids, MI: Eerdmans, 2010).

4. C. S. Lewis, *Surprised by Joy: The Shape of My Early Life* (New York: Harcourt Brace, 1956).

Chapter 6

The Wizard of Oz

WHEN JUSTINE SACCO got off the plane she was the most hated person in the world.

Eleven hours earlier Justine was about to board her very long plane flight to Africa. Killing time in the airport she was firing off snarky jokes on Twitter for her 170 Twitter followers, mostly family and friends. She sent one last tweet, one more edgy joke, before getting on the plane for the eleven-hour flight.

When Justine landed eleven hours later, she turned on her phone to discover that she had been fired and that the whole world hated her.

The last joke Justine uploaded to Twitter was: "Going to Africa. Hope I don't get AIDS. Just kidding. I'm white!"

Not the funniest joke about white privilege, and one, most definitely, that crossed the lines of political correctness. It seemed that the joke fell flat with her 170 Twitter followers. No one responded.

And that's where things might have ended, with a poor, tasteless attempt at humor among friends, lost forever among the billions of ignored tweets. Except that Justine Sacco's poor joke was retweeted by one journalist with a large following. And then retweeted. And retweeted again. On the flight she was blissfully unaware about the social media storm that was engulfing her. By the time she landed, Justine Sacco was the number one worldwide trend on Twitter.

When she got off the plane in Africa, Justine Sacco was the most infamous person on Twitter.[1]

The outrage over Sacco's tweet was unanimous in its verdict: the joke was disgusting, racist, and cruel (even though she'd meant it as a backhanded jab at her own privilege). What sort of monster would ever say such a thing? People wanted to know!

Due to the social media firestorm during her flight, the tweet came to the attention of her employer. He took to Twitter to publicly fire her. A chorus of cheers broke out on social media.

Flying high above it all, Sacco had no idea that her sad attempt at a joke had just ruined her life.

You might have heard about Justine Sacco's story. But even if you haven't, you've surely seen or heard about "Twitter storms" or "social media mobs" where thousands (or dozens) of people use social media to denounce and shame a person who has done something that offends our collective sense of right and wrong. Long ago, when it came to public shaming, you wore a scarlet letter. Today, it's a hashtag that goes viral.

While it's easy to denounce the mob rule of Twitter, it's also important to point out the moral aspect of these Twitter firestorms. People weren't outraged about Sacco's Tweet because it was a comedic misfire, they were outraged because they perceived the joke to be cruel, insensitive, and racist; and we tend to think it's important, if we want to make the world a better place, to call out and denounce cruelty, insensitivity, and racism.

The people who mobbed Justine Sacco on Twitter that day thought they were doing the right thing, that if we worked together

---

1. Jon Ronson, *So You've Been Publicly Shamed* (New York: Riverhead, 2015).

to shame people like her, perhaps the world will be less cruel and insensitive.

Maybe. Or we might ruin a person's life for making one ill-judged joke.

Perhaps in our rush to make the world less cruel and insensitive we actually made it more so. The righteousness of the Twitter mob that ruined Justine Sacco's life is a cautionary tale. As Friedrich Nietzsche famously warned, "Whoever fights monsters should see to it that in the process he does not become a monster."

Talking More about Spiritual Warfare

Spiritual warfare is a battle between good and evil if we focus exclusively on the *spiritual* element. But what happens to doubting and disenchanted Christians is that the *spiritual* element is rejected or ignored in favor of a completely *political* vision. *Spiritual* warfare is routinely traded in for *political* warfare. And in political warfare the battle becomes very much about "flesh and blood," about defeating the Bad People. People like Justine Sacco. So the mob forms, picking up their Twitter pitchforks. The Angels of Light go marching off to war. We want to fight things like racism but in the process we end up attacking human beings and ruining their lives. And it's this violence against human beings that a vision of spiritual warfare is trying to prevent.

Critics of spiritual warfare have got it backwards when they say that talking about demons will cause you to demonize other human beings. The truth is that it's the exact opposite: it's our *refusal* to talk about demons that causes us to demonize other human beings.

The reason for this should be pretty obvious. If there isn't a spiritual dynamic at work in the struggle, if the struggle for social justice is thoroughly disenchanted, then it's destined to be a battle against other human beings, against the Bad People—the Good People trying to wrest power away from the Bad People. When spiritual warfare loses its spiritual component our battle can't help but become against flesh and blood.

That's the predictable and violent outcome that *spiritual* warfare prevents. Spiritual warfare *saves us from violence*. And if the violence here isn't physical violence, then it is most certainly *psychological* violence, the way our crusades for righteousness can dehumanize people like Justine Sacco.

Again the ironies abound. By disenchanting our vision of spiritual warfare—reducing it to a human, political struggle—doubting and disenchanted Christians are perennially tempted to demonize the Bad Guys, to turn political opponents into monsters. Without a spiritual target and location of struggle where our anger can be directed, social justice reduces to a political battle against evil human beings. I think that's why our political discourse has become so hostile and violent: spiritual virtues and weapons such as confession, self-control, repentance, humility, peacemaking, forgiveness, joy, mercy, and love have all gone missing. A disenchanted political struggle is reduced to a bloody, winner-take-all cage match.

More (Spiritual) Warfare = Less (Physical) Violence

For followers of Jesus, spiritual warfare isn't just about the struggle for *justice*. It's also the struggle to *love*.

Love is what makes Jesus so attractive, his love for the broken, rejected, oppressed, and marginalized. But the love of Jesus also interrupts us. Beyond loving lepers and prostitutes, Jesus also loved the agents of an oppressive empire—Jewish tax collectors and Roman centurions. Our hearts thrill to how Jesus loved the oppressed, but things get more complicated when Jesus preaches love for oppressors in the Sermon on the Mount:

> "You have heard that it was said, 'Eye for eye, and tooth for tooth.' But I tell you, do not resist an evil person. If anyone slaps you on the right cheek, turn to them the other cheek also. And if anyone wants to sue you and take your shirt, hand over your

coat as well. If anyone forces you to go one mile, go with them two miles. Give to the one who asks you, and do not turn away from the one who wants to borrow from you.

"You have heard that it was said, 'Love your neighbor and hate your enemy.' But I tell you, love your enemies and pray for those who persecute you, that you may be children of your Father in heaven. He causes his sun to rise on the evil and the good, and sends rain on the righteous and the unrighteous. If you love those who love you, what reward will you get? Are not even the tax collectors doing that? And if you greet only your own people, what are you doing more than others? Do not even pagans do that? Be perfect, therefore, as your heavenly Father is perfect. (Matthew 5:38-48)

Everyone in Jesus' audience knew who the enemy was: the Roman oppressors and their Jewish surrogates. They were the ones forcing people to carry their bag a mile, the ones doing the persecuting, the ones striking people on the face.

In the face of those aggressions, Jesus says, "Love your enemies." Love the oppressors *and* the oppressed. Being like God, Jesus says, means loving all people, indiscriminately.

If our political struggle for justice is to resist the temptations toward dehumanization and hatred, it must be accompanied by this deeper spiritual struggle to love our enemies. Love is what prevents the political struggle from dehumanizing and demonizing flesh and blood.

But this is hard work, because when you care passionately about injustice you're going to get angry. And if we're also loving our enemies, where are we going to direct that anger? In the struggle for justice passions run hot, especially on social media, where it's easier to demonize and dehumanize the Justine Sacco's of the world. If spiritual warfare is anything, it's the struggle to find room for both love and anger in the very same heart. As you can imagine, this is quite an emotional trick to pull off.

And the Rage Shall Lie Down with the Love

And that trick is spiritual warfare. Spiritual warfare *energizes your anger* but *lovingly redirects that anger* away from human beings and toward a common enemy. Spiritual warfare gives us a vision of how human beings can become captives to larger unseen forces that trap us in perpetual conflict. We come to see how all of us are being manipulated as pawns in a larger game, a game that is continually pushing us toward violent, hateful confrontation. Focusing upon those larger forces creates a capacity for mercy. We follow Jesus' example as he prayed from the cross, "Father forgive them, for they do not know what they are doing." Jesus finds mercy for those who killed him because he saw them as leaves being blown about by violent winds—political, social, cultural, psychological, and historical winds.

I like how N. T. Wright describes the dark forces in the world that can blow us around, how despite our doubts and disenchantment these forces are still recognizably at work in the world today, still exerting an influence on human affairs. Wright writes:

> The modern world divides into those who are obsessed with demonic powers and those who mock them as outdated rubbish. Neither approach . . . does justice to reality. . . . Despite the caricatures, the obsession, and the sheer muddle that people often get themselves into on this subject, there is such a thing as a dark force that seems to take over people, movements, and sometimes whole countries, a force or (as it sometimes seems) a set of forces that can make people do things they would never normally do.
>
> You might have thought the history of the twentieth century would provide plenty of examples of this [i.e., a dark force taking over people, movements, and countries], but many still choose to resist the conclusion—despite the increasing use in

public life of the language of "force" (economic "forces," political "forces," peer "pressure," and so on).[2]

Wright goes on to affirm my point that when we recognize these forces at work in human affairs it allows us to humanize enemies and oppressors. We can come to see the people we are fighting against as not intrinsically evil but as victims and pawns of these larger, unseen forces. We can come to see that the evil we are fighting against can trap us all, blurring the lines between the Good Guys and the Bad Guys. We start to wonder if the righteous Twitter mob I'm joining is as righteous as it appears to be.

We learn that in our crusade against the forces of darkness the Devil is always appearing to us as an Angel of Light.

That's what Lucifer means after all.

Lucifer means Angel of *Light*.

Just Remember That Ant

We don't have to get overly spooky when we think of these forces. All we need to recognize now is that there are unseen, impersonal forces in the world that can't be located in time or space, forces that are perpetually pulling us into darkness, forces prowling the world like a lion looking for someone to devour.

And if you're still struggling to get your head around that notion, let me share two metaphors that might help.

Think of an ant colony. No single ant has the blueprint of the ant colony in its head. No one ant is running the show, directing the ants to forage, build, or defend the colony—all these things happen with no one running the show or calling the shots. What we observe from on high, looking down at the ant colony as a whole, is order and pattern, an order and pattern that, once established, has

---

2. N. T. Wright, *Simply Jesus: Who He Was, What He Did, Why It Matters* (New York: HarperOne, 2011), 121–22.

causal effects upon the individual ants, directing and organizing their behaviors. A pattern emerges from the parts and then exerts a downward force upon those parts. The whole is greater than the sum of its parts.

But this causal force can't be located in or reduced to any of the parts being affected. If you could ask the ants, "Who's in charge here?" they'd be stumped. No single ant is the Wizard of Oz running the show behind a curtain. Instead, the Wizard is everywhere, an unseen force at work in every microscopic interaction between the ants, organizing and directing their behavior. And the Wizard of Oz is much older than the ants. As the lives of ants begin and end, the pattern organizing them persists, outliving the individual ants.

The ants die. But the Wizard lives on.

Or think of a cloud. A cloud is a structure that emerges from a collection of individual water molecules. Clouds can't be reduced to those water molecules, but clouds, once they exist, start bossing around those water molecules, throwing them around in thunderstorms and hurricanes.

Similar things happen with human beings and societies, forces that sweep through human history on large and small scales. Like water molecules, people are sucked into a dark vortex, a moral tempest, a thunderstorm.

Consider the rise of Nazism leading up to World War II. As a moral force, it was bigger than Hitler—Nazism can't be reduced to Hitler. And once Nazism got traction, it became a moral thunderstorm in human affairs, sucking more and more air molecules into the vortex. Nazism became the Wizard. Nazism took on a life of its own. In fact, Hitler has been dead for over seventy years and Nazism *still* plagues the world. Hitler himself—as a memory, as an idea, as moral and spiritual force—continues to exert a perverse moral influence upon human affairs—he lives on as a dark angel haunting humanity.

Once we come to reckon with something like Nazism as a moral force, we can entertain some empathy for those who were caught up in the storm. Have you wondered how you would have responded if you'd lived in Germany at the time? I'd like to think I would have behaved nobly and heroically, but more likely I would have been vulnerable to the temptations of the Wizard. And in the recognition of this vulnerability lies the potential for empathy. We can come to see how people *just like me* can get blinded to and caught up in some pretty nasty and evil things. This isn't to go soft on Nazism. Quite the opposite. Our rage is directed *at* Nazism. Full force. But because we love, our goal is *liberating human beings* from their slavery to this spiritual power. To rescue them from the Wizard. Our battle is not against flesh and blood but against the spiritual *forces* of wickedness.

This is how a vision of spiritual warfare can help deflect hatred away from human beings to fight the Wizard. We can see oppressors as human beings, as vulnerable to evil the same way I am vulnerable to evil. Our battles for justice can be focused upon the unseen satanic aspect rather than upon the flesh and blood of human beings.

Thinking back to what happened to Justine Sacco and the shaming of people on social media, it's interesting how we talk about forces. We talk about Twitter "mobs" and "storms," a social media hurricane that pulls us in, like a thundercloud sucking in water molecules to grow larger and larger.

I doubt that the people who retweeted Sacco's poor joke wanted to ruin her life. They were trying to make the world a better and more humane place. And really, what difference is one retweet going to make? It's such a little inconsequential thing, your small part to call out insensitivity and racism in the world. Really, what power does one ant have?

But the little things add up, things start trending, and more and more of us are pulled into the social media maelstrom. A mob forms and the Angels of Light go marching off to war again.

And that's what happens when we're trying to do the *right* thing! Consider all the little things that add up to create systemic racism or damage the environment. Little ants doing little things, ants trying to do the right thing or ants just obliviously going about their business.

We'd like to grab an ant and yell, "Hey, the world's falling apart! People are getting hurt! Who's in charge here?" But the ant can't say. So we team up with the good ants to gang up on the bad ants. With no Wizard behind the curtain, it's just a battle of ant against ant.

But the Wizard is there, unseen and always at work.

Chapter 7

I Love Humanity. It's People I Can't Stand!

ONE OF MY favorite *Peanuts* comic strips is one when Linus, after an altercation with Lucy, screams, "I love mankind . . . it's *people* I can't stand!!"

I can identify. Conceptually, philosophically, politically, theologically, and emotionally, well, I love humanity. Humanity has no bigger fan. But *actual* human beings? The individuals in my life with names? That, not so much. Actual human beings are often irritating, demanding, inconvenient, or boring. I love the *idea* of people more than *actual* people.

And social media makes it all so much worse. We can post to Facebook or Twitter a passionate plea about a humanitarian crisis going on in the world and then, once we've shut the laptop, step back into our comfortable lives and routines. True, we might feel distressed through the day, carrying the sorrow with us about what is going on in the world. But let's be honest. Outrage, compassion, and sorrow are *feelings*. Good feelings, no doubt, but feelings aren't actions. And most importantly, when it comes to loving people feelings aren't *relationships*.

I have a lot of Christian friends who talk a lot about poverty who have never invited a homeless person into their home. It's so very easy to love "the homeless" in the abstract, as an idea. It's easy to love "the homeless" on Facebook, at the voting booth, or in a theological discussion. But inviting people off the street into your home? That's a whole other ballgame.

The Pointless Church

In his book *Kingdom Conspiracy* Scot McKnight talks about "skinny jeans" Christians, his term for younger, socially conscious Christians. According to McKnight, for these "skinny jeans" Christians the kingdom of God means "good deeds done by good people (Christian or not) in the public sector for the common good."[1] As he notes, given their focus on social justice these "skinny jeans" Christians have "turned the kingdom message of Jesus into a politically shaped message."[2]

There are many reasons why "skinny jeans" Christians have equated the political pursuit of social justice with what Jesus called the "kingdom of God." One of the reasons is doubt and disenchantment among the "skinny jeans" crowd. Making God's kingdom come "on earth as it is in heaven," to echo Jesus in the Lord's Prayer, is creating a more humane, just, and peaceable world. And this vision works just fine in a disenchanted world, free of demons and angels.

---

1. Scot McKnight, *Kingdom Conspiracy: Returning to the Radical Mission of the Local Church* (Grand Rapids, MI: Brazos, 2014), 4.
2. Ibid.

But disenchantment isn't the only reason why this "doing good deeds for the common good" vision of the kingdom has become so attractive. Younger Christians have grown increasingly disillusioned with the institutional church. This is especially the case for post-fundamentalist and post-evangelical Christians who've been hurt by the church. And even if you haven't been burned by a church, in a world full of suffering, pain, and injustice it can be hard to see the point of going to church to sing some songs, eat some dough-nuts, and listen to a lecture about an ancient book full of violence and backward views about gender and sexuality. Even if church isn't toxic, it's definitely pointless and irrelevant.

Plus, rarely does the church seem to act like Jesus. The church doesn't seem to be interested in Jesus' radical embrace of sinners and prostitutes or the prophetic call to "Let justice roll down like a river!" If anything, the church—now and historically—has actively *inter-fered* with the pursuit of Jesus and justice in the world.

So *kingdom* is a word that is increasingly being used to separate the work of God in the world from the traditional *church*. *King-dom* means "good deeds done for the common good" while *church* means, well, going to church on a Sunday morning to sing songs, listen to a sermon, and drink bad coffee. This clean separation between *kingdom* and *church* allows us to blow off the church—as being irrelevant, corrupt, or toxic—to pursue the kingdom of God in the world, partnering with others (Christians or not) in making the world a better place.

Also, kingdom work seems so much more heroic, making an actual difference in the world. Kingdom work *is saving lives*. Dig-ging a well in Africa seems a better use of our time than standing around drinking bad coffee at church. Kingdom work is Jesus-work. Going to church? Not so much.

And because kingdom work is public work for the common good, we can partner with anyone in this diverse and pluralistic world. It doesn't matter if you're an atheist or a Muslim, if you want to help me dig a well in Africa we can do that together, as partners.

Kingdom work unifies us. Church, by contrast, draws a line in the sand between us and the world. Where kingdom work embraces diversity in our shared work for the common good, church seems exclusive and judgmental. By focusing on good deeds done in the world, the kingdom vision is inherently tolerant and inclusive. It's all hands on deck, no judgment, which seems so much more like Jesus than the judgmental piety and hypocrisy of the traditional church.

So the kingdom vision is a heroic, inclusive vision, making a real difference in the world. And the traditional church just can't compete. There's nothing all that heroic about rolling out of bed early on Sunday morning, going to church to sing some praise songs, and drinking bad coffee—at least not while there are starving children in Africa.

Drinking Bad Coffee to Save the World

And yet, Jesus wasn't much of a political activist, but what Jesus did do—and the early church followed his lead—was to create a community characterized by two things: the practices of *care* and *peace*. People flocked to Jesus because he cared for them. He healed them, protected them, honored them, included them, blessed them, and fed them.

And the early church continued these practices of care. In the earliest descriptions of the church in Acts 2 and 4 we see them caring for each other, to the point of selling their possessions, so that there was no hungry or homeless or lonely person among them. Over and over in the epistles, the church is encouraged to care for and love each other, in concrete and tangible ways. There are too many texts to cite, but here are a few. This is what church is supposed to be like:

Romans 12:9
Be devoted to one another in love. Honor one another above yourselves.

Ephesians 4:2
Be completely humble and gentle; be patient, bearing with one another in love.

Philippians 2:2-4
Do nothing out of selfish ambition or vain conceit. Rather, in humility value others above yourselves, not looking to your own interests but each of you to the interests of the others.

1 John 3:16
This is how we know what love is: Jesus Christ laid down his life for us. And we ought to lay down our lives for our brothers and sisters.

1 Corinthians 12:24-26
But God has put the body together, giving greater honor to the parts that lacked it, so that there should be no division in the body, but that its parts should have equal concern for each other. If one part suffers, every part suffers with it; if one part is honored, every part rejoices with it.

The church is a laboratory of love, a place where material care, sharing, hospitality, and mutual honoring are practiced and lived out.

In addition to care, Jesus also practiced peace. In Jesus' band of followers were Zealots and a tax collector, sworn enemies of one another. Jesus, a Jew, cared for Samaritans and colonial occupiers. Following Jesus, the early church was revolutionary in how it broke down the "wall of hostility" that had existed between Jew and Gentile. The church is also a laboratory of peace:

Romans 12:18
If it is possible, as far as it depends on you, live at peace with everyone.

Romans 14:19
Let us therefore make every effort to do what leads to peace and to mutual edification.

2 Corinthians 13:11
Finally, brothers and sisters, rejoice! Strive for full restoration, encourage one another, be of one mind, live in peace. And the God of love and peace will be with you.

Ephesians 4:3
Make every effort to keep the unity of the Spirit through the bond of peace.

Colossians 3:15
Let the peace of Christ rule in your hearts, since as members of one body you were called to peace.

1 Thessalonians 5:13
Live in peace with each other.

Hebrews 12:14
Make every effort to live in peace with everyone and to be holy; without holiness no one will see the Lord.

This is just a small sample of all the exhortations to practice peace, to say nothing of the exhortations to forgive and extend mercy or the exhortations for unity and reconciliation.

Repeatedly, the Bible tells us that the church is the place where we come together to practice *care* and *peace*. The church is a laboratory of love and reconciliation, a workshop of sharing and forgiving, a testing ground of mercy and grace.

And what is vitally important about all this is how care and peace are practices being worked out face-to-face with real people. The kingdom of God is the hard, intimate, and sweaty work of simply getting along with people. The church is the laboratory of care and peace where you can't get away with loving humanity abstractly and theoretically. You have to practice care and peace with the person standing right in front of you, the person boring you or annoying you as you're sipping bad coffee together.

Jesus didn't leave behind a political party. Jesus gave us a group of people to get along with.

And while that might seem simple enough, if you've ever tried caring for and living at peace with a group of people, you know it's one of the hardest things in the world. It's much easier to love people in the abstract than to love actual human beings. But that's what the church gives you: actual human beings.

For example, before I started sharing life at Freedom and going out to the prison, like a lot of liberals I cared about poverty abstractly and theoretically, as a political and theological *issue*. And when you talk about poverty at a distance, theologically and politically, you can get sort of romantic about "the poor." But as anyone who's lived life on the socioeconomic margins will tell you, poverty is often ugly and sharing life there is hard work. It's messy, complicated, inconvenient, and heartbreaking. Again, loving actual faces and names is difficult for us. And a lot of fired-up-for-social-justice Christians discover they just don't have the stomach for it. It's a whole lot easier to love "the poor" on Facebook than it is to be in relationship with actual people day in and day out.

Hard Work in the Laboratory of Love

I've had people in the grip of an addiction lie to me and manipulate me. I've driven people home to discover they have bed bugs. We've had homeless people in our house, but once my wife Jana and I entertained a guest with a hygiene problem so bad we feared the furniture would be ruined. Some people lack the social graces that make time together fun and enjoyable. This laboratory of love is no easy thing.

The same goes for my time at the prison. It's easy to romanticize prison ministry, but it can be difficult at times. Some of the strongest Christians I know attend our Bible study, but not everyone who comes loves Jesus. Prison is boring, so some men attend just for something to do and the air-conditioning in the chapel. And as a part of your regular training to work in the volunteer programs at the prison, you're put on alert about all the ways the inmates might try to use you for their own advantage. And prison is full of sociopathic people. Which puts you on edge and makes you suspicious and wary at times. So it's hard work in that laboratory of love.

I'm doing the same work on Sunday morning at my church. Just because most of us have day jobs doesn't mean we don't have issues. On the surface, sure, we all look well dressed and put together. But if you've spent any time at all talking to people over bad coffee at church you've seen the vast reservoirs of pain, loneliness, shame, and insecurity welling up behind our eyes. Recently I looked out over my Bible class at church. I saw a single Latina mom, desperately lonely and looking for friends. I saw a man whose wife just filed for a divorce. Another who just lost his job. I saw a mother weeping because her middle-aged son was dying of cancer. I saw the parents who will be visiting their adopted son in prison that week. I saw my friend Karen, blind and sitting in a wheelchair, knowing how lonely she feels living in an assisted-living facility.

And then there's me. Filled with my own sin, darkness, and brokenness.

That's church. Just an ordinary group of people who gather each week to participate in the liturgy of drinking bad coffee together, the liturgy where we practice the hard, awkward, and intimate work of caring for each other. A liturgy so powerful, transformative, and holy that even atheists are starting to gather on Sunday mornings in "Sunday assemblies" to experience it.

Drinking bad coffee is saving the world.

Drinking Bad Coffee to Defeat Satan

When we love humanity in the abstract, like loving humanity on social media or through a political party, one of the things that's persistently hidden from us is our own inner darkness, our own spiritual poverty and brokenness—our inner demons. Community, real community, involves exposure. Only community can reveal, surface, and unmask our inner brokenness and sinfulness.

This spiritual exposure is ultimately what we're trying to avoid when we trade the church for political and social media activism, it's the exposure we're avoiding when we trade the church for shared pints of beer and good meals with likeminded friends. True community brings us into contact with people who expose our jealousies, impatience, intolerance, pettiness, selfishness, and vanity. Consequently, persisting and sticking with community—what the monastic tradition calls a vow of stability, the covenantal promise to stick with each other through thick and thin—is a spiritual discipline where you are working out your salvation with fear and trembling.

My guiding light here is Jean Vanier, founder of the L'Arche community. L'Arche is comprised of communities where people live and share life with those who have intellectual and physical disabilities. Henri Nouwen, the famous Christian author, left his life as a professor at Harvard to live with a L'Arche community.

When I think of the relationship between church and spiritual warfare I often think about this quote from Jean Vanier:

> Community is the place where our limitations, our fears and our egotism are revealed to us. We discover our poverty and our weaknesses, our inability to get on with some people, our mental and emotional blocks, our affective and sexual disturbances, our seemingly insatiable desires, our frustrations and jealousies, our hatred and our wish to destroy. While we are alone, we could believe we loved everyone. Now that we are with others, living with them all the time, we realise how incapable we are of loving, how much we deny to others, how closed in on ourselves we are.[3]

This is why church is a form of spiritual warfare. When we are alone, loving the world through Facebook and Twitter, it's easy to convince ourselves that we love everyone. In community, however, our inability to love is exposed, along with our inability to get along with some people. It's community that leads us to confess: "I love humanity. It's people I can't stand."

This is why church is ground zero for spiritual warfare. All those biblical commands to care and live at peace? They were aimed at scattered and small Christian communities just trying to get along with each other. People who knew each other on a first-name basis.

---

3. Jean Vanier, *Community and Growth*, 2nd rev. edition (New York: Paulist, 1989), 26.

It's not too much of an exaggeration to say that Jesus' kingdom vision was focused almost exclusively on getting these communities to simply share life together, to care for each other, day in and day out, in concrete and tangible ways. And the mission they were given is the same mission we are given: become an intimate, face-to-face community of care and peace. That's what Jesus called the kingdom of God.

While all this doesn't make community sound very appealing, that's just because I've been describing the side that involves spiritual discipline and struggle. True, community exposes my spiritual brokenness, but the unexpected joy and grace we receive in community far outweigh the hard and annoying things. Sharing life at Freedom and out at the prison isn't easy, but I'm continually interrupted by grace and surprised by joy. Like the night at Freedom when I witnessed Jeffery's gift.

Jeffery's Gift

When I pulled up to Karen's assisted-living facility, Jeffery was standing on the curb holding an invitation to our meal and worship service at Freedom. Jeffery was waiting on the church van, but it hadn't come. So he was getting worried and agitated. Talking with Jeffery, who has cognitive disabilities, I couldn't tell if he'd made arrangements with the van. I guessed that Jeffery didn't know he had to call the church ahead of time to arrange for a ride.

But no matter. I was there to pick up Karen for our meal and praise service, and Jeffery could come with us. We went in to inform the nursing staff that Jeffery would be coming with me for the evening. Jeffery helped me push Karen to the car and get her wheelchair loaded into the trunk, and then we were off.

Being in an unfamiliar place, Jeffery wanted me close throughout the dinner. Afterwards, during the service, Jeffery was alternately engaged and discomfited by everything we were doing. He wanted to participate but seemed at times scared and unsure of himself. During a time of prayer he asked me to pray for him. I laid hands on him and prayed over him. And then I asked if Jeffery would pray for me. He followed my example and laid hands on me and mumbled words of a prayer. I couldn't make out what he was saying. But when he finished he looked up at me with moist eyes, on the edge of tears. Whatever he'd said, he'd meant, and he'd been moved by it.

During communion Jeffery again grew scared and hesitant. He didn't want to go down front with Karen and me to participate.

And then the prayer for the offering came. Jeffery's agitation grew. He knew what was coming—the passing of collection baskets—and he knew he wanted to give but didn't have any money. Jeffery leaned over to tell me this with some concern. I gently reassured Jeffery that he didn't have to give any money.

But that reassurance didn't seem to help. So I asked Jeffery if I could share some of my money with him. No, that wasn't what he wanted. He wanted to have something of his own to give.

The baskets passed in front of us. Jeffery seemed sad and distraught about what to do. The attendants moved past our row.

And then I saw Jeffery calm. A peace seemed to fall over him.

He'd decided on something.

As the baskets passed behind us he turned in his seat and solemnly took off his baseball hat.

And then he placed his hat in the collection basket.

The baskets were taken up. The collection was finished. Jeffery turned to me, beaming.

"I gave my hat," he said with a huge smile.

I beamed back, with tears in my eyes. "I saw, Jeffery, I saw."

He leaned over for a hug.

We hugged. And rejoiced in his gift.

Community is hard. And Jeffery, you should know, isn't always so easy to get along with. There are days when he's agitated and he'll call me a dozen times. He doesn't know any better, but that doesn't make it any easier to have my phone ringing all day at work.

But that night at Freedom, Jeffery's generosity interrupted me and in ways that I will carry forever. I was changed that night. Wherever I struggle with giving, sharing, or generosity, I always think of Jeffery's gift.

Maybe now you will as well.

Of course, you know, we stood around that night at Freedom drinking bad coffee.

We always do. Karen takes her coffee with cream and sugar. So does Jeffery. I just take cream.

Our shared liturgy of bad coffee, saving us, drop by drop.

Chapter 8

God at War

A VOLUME OF very dark poetry sits on my shelf. Years ago, after I had received my master's degree in psychology I took a job working in a psychiatric hospital, and I worked there for four years. And throughout those years I wrote poetry, some very dark and gloomy poetry, filling page after page in a blank journal. Here's a taste:

behind
the veneer
of our lives
the hollowness
of us
rumbles
ignored
covered
and masked by our noise

Not the greatest verse in the world, but I wanted you to get a taste of the bleakness.

I don't think I knew what I was doing at the time, but I see now what was going on. I started the journal soon after I started working at the hospital, and I stopped writing the day I left. That was not a coincidence. I see now how I was using that journal to cope with the vast ocean of suffering I was being exposed to on a daily basis. I needed an emotional outlet, and writing that poetry helped me process what I was experiencing. The enormity of the pain I witnessed and waded into was beyond what my heart could bear: the bandaged wrists from suicide attempts; unimaginable and horrific accounts of sexual abuse; the walking skeletons of anorexia; the hell of depression; the brain damage of addiction; the broken minds of psychosis. The hospital was an ever-changing kaleidoscope of human pain and suffering, each day revealing in sharp relief a new and traumatic pattern.

I remember one evening sitting all night in the doorway of a woman who was on suicide watch. I read *Walden* that night while she peacefully slept. A few days later she was discharged. The insurance company didn't want to pay for any more in-patient care. It was too expensive.

A week later at lunch a friend at the hospital pushed the newspaper across the table toward me. He tapped the obituary section. I saw the woman's name. We'd discharged her. And she killed herself.

And each day after work I'd fill my journal with dark poetry.

Though I wasn't aware of it at the time, I started losing my faith during those years in the hospital. The suffering overwhelmed me. My heart was broken. And God didn't seem to care. During the years I was writing in the journal I stopped praying, and I didn't pray again for many years.

It's no accident that my faith faltered during the years I wrote poetry in that journal. As I noted in chapter 2, compassion can erode our faith. Compassion is what draws us to Jesus and to the suffering of the world. But the pain we encounter there places an enormous burden upon our faith. We scream to the heavens: *Where are you God in the midst of all this pain? Don't you see? Don't you care?*

Compassion makes faith a heavy burden to bear. It's hard to believe when your heart gets broken, broken over and over again by the pain of the world.

In the years since my work in the hospital my faith has stabilized. While I still have doubts and I still struggle with disenchantment—even with the Holy Ghost conga lines out at Freedom—my faith has returned and grown deeper roots. A key reason for this is that I figured out why my compassion had been eroding rather than energizing my faith: I was lacking a theology of spiritual warfare.

As Greg Boyd argues in his book *God at War*, when doubting and disenchanted Christians lose touch with the warfare worldview of the Bible, we begin to treat the suffering of the world like it's a logical puzzle to be solved rather than a reality to be resisted.[1] And when we treat suffering as an intellectual problem, all that happens is that our doubts and questions pile up. Our mind starts running in a circle, chasing its own tail.

But very much unlike us, the Bible seems untroubled by the presence of pain, suffering, evil, and brokenness in the world. Across the pages of the Bible, evil and suffering are simply assumed to exist. Suffering exists and we must act—that's the starting point. *Evil and suffering exist, do something!* That's the warfare worldview, and that is the only thing the Bible seems interested in communicating to us.

Consequently, the existence of evil doesn't seem to pose any theological problem in the Bible—not in the Old Testament, not for Jesus in the Gospels, and not for the early church. The biblical writers cry out to God in the face of oppression, injustice, and violence, beseeching God to act in history to rescue the weak and victimized. But the *existence* of evil isn't the focal point of lament, only *God's inaction* in the face of evil. The Bible is notoriously uninterested in providing us a theodicy—that is, a theological account of why evil

1. Gregory A. Boyd, *God at War: The Bible & Spiritual Conflict* (Downers Grove, IL: InterVarsity, 1997).

exists. Evil is simply taken as a given—a given to be resisted. Boyd calls this a *theology of revolt*. The biblical response to evil isn't *philosophical* but *behavioral*. We might phrase it this way: The only theodicy we find in the Bible is *resistance*. A theology of revolt trades in philosophical bafflement for boots on the ground.

As doubts about the existence of Old Scratch have increased in our disenchanted and secular age, so has our ability to imagine and embrace the warfare worldview of the Bible. And with the loss of this imagination we've grown unable to articulate and practice a theology of revolt in the face of suffering. Rather than assuming the world is a battleground—where Hades is crashing into the gates of the kingdom of God—and jumping into the thick of the struggle, we swamp ourselves with questions the Bible just doesn't seem interested in answering. And even though many of these questions flow out of our compassion, without a posture of revolt our compassion compounds our doubts instead of energizing our faith. Lacking a theology of revolt, faith gets overloaded with doubt and eventually sinks.

Ultimately it was a theology of revolt that helped me recover my faith. In the face of suffering I had turned *inward*. Instead of *acting* I became *introspective*. Instead of standing with the suffering in the world, I'd read a theology book to get some answers. I was crippled and overwhelmed by theological questions regarding the origins of evil and the nature of God. I'd turned suffering into a logical puzzle.

And for years I banged my head against the wall, trying to crack the problem. But eventually it dawned on me that I was expending enormous amounts of mental and emotional energy that could be put to much better use. So I shelved my doubts and headed out to the prison. I started cleaning up after the community meals at Freedom where we feed hungry and homeless neighbors. I could sit around debating the problem of evil or I could do the dishes.

I chose the dishes.

I turned the corner in my faith when I adopted a theology of revolt, a vision of spiritual warfare, a posture of action over theological rumination. I got disgusted with how much time and energy I was wasting on my doubts. It was time to get off my theological ass and into the game.

The world is suffering. And in the face of that suffering Jesus went about doing good and healing all those under the power of the devil.

God is at war. And it's time for us to join the fight.

PART 3

A Great Campaign of Sabotage

Spiritual Warfare for Doubters and the Disenchanted

Chapter 9

"Get Behind Me, Satan!"

WHEN FRED PHELPS died in 2014, the church he founded in 1955, the infamous Westboro Baptist Church, claimed it had picketed more than 53,000 events. From Lady Gaga concerts to funerals of fallen U.S. soldiers to locations of natural disasters to sites of school shootings, a typical Westboro demonstration would include a handful of church members, often with small children, brandishing signs that read "God Hates Fags" and "God Is Your Enemy."

There persists a worry, both inside and outside Christianity, about any purported vision that might go by the label "spiritual warfare." Religious fundamentalisms abound and they often show a hateful, intolerant, and violent face. And behind those fundamentalisms sits a dualistic vision of the world where Angels of Light are doing battle against the Forces of Darkness. The worry is that the inevitable trajectory of any vision of spiritual warfare is Fred Phelps and Westboro Baptist Church. Spiritual warfare, it is assumed, must involve some hostility between God and humanity, an antagonism that allows us to join God's holy crusade against the wicked people in the world. And once that seed of hostility is planted there's nothing to stop it from growing into the hatred and vitriol displayed by people like Fred Phelps and his church. While most Christians won't take it to the Westboro extreme, the difference is simply a matter of degree.

If we're going to deal with spiritual warfare, we've got to reckon with the specter of a Fred Phelps. We need to get a clear handle on how Christianity can take such a tragic turn. We need a clear-eyed assessment of what goes wrong with Christians who begin to use God as a weapon against others. Because we need to determine, right at the start, if there is something inherently problematic with the notion of spiritual warfare or if the problem is located elsewhere.

As a psychologist, I like to think that all the great psychological theories began with the words, "There are two kinds of people in the world," grand statements that attempt to bring to light some important contrast between people. So indulge me: There are two kinds of Christians in the world, there are *Two Love Christians* and *One Love Christians*. And understanding the difference explains why there are Christians like Fred Phelps and Westboro Baptist Church and how spiritual warfare can stay well clear of that tragic outcome.

Jesus famously amended the Shema of ancient Israel. Everyday the Israelites would recite the Shema, the fundamental creed of their faith:

> Hear, O Israel: The Lord our God, the Lord is one. Love the Lord your God with all your heart and with all your soul and with all your strength.

Love the Lord your God, that was the prime directive. But some questions needed answering. Yes, love the Lord, but what does this love entail? How is this love practiced? How are we to love the Lord? These were questions that were hotly debated by the rabbis.

Jesus entered this contentious debate by appending another commandment to the Shema. Here's how it's recorded in the Gospel of Matthew:

"Teacher, which is the greatest commandment in the Law?"

Jesus replied: " 'Love the Lord your God with all your heart and with all your soul and with all your mind.' This is the first and greatest commandment. And the second is like it: 'Love your neighbor as yourself.' All the Law and the Prophets hang on these two commandments." (Matthew 22:36-40)

In addition to the Shema (Deuteronomy 6:4-5) Jesus adds Leviticus 19:18: "Love your neighbor as yourself." These two we call the "Greatest Commandments"—according to Jesus, loving God is conflated and mixed up with loving human beings.

Now, this conflation might seem straightforward and simple to understand, but this is also where things can start to go wrong, and terribly wrong at that. Christians have been debating Jesus' mixture of loves—loving God, loving people—for two millennia, and often with tragic outcomes. Christians disagree about how we are to mix and balance these commands to love God and our neighbors: Is Jesus saying that there are *two* loves—a love directed at God and a love directed at people? If there are two loves, they might come into conflict at some point. For example, because we love God and want to please and obey God, our obedience to God might cause us to be less loving toward human beings. In the Two Loves view, our ultimate loyalty is to God, so our love of God must trump our love for human beings. Christians like Fred Phelps and Westboro Baptist Church display the extreme outcome of the Two Loves view, a sad and tragic example of how a purported "love of God" comes to justify hatred toward human beings. Whenever you hear someone say that they love God more than human beings watch out, because that person is about to hurt somebody. In *the name of God* they are planning to hurt somebody.

That's the inherent danger of the Two Loves view of the Greatest Commandments, the possibility that the love of God can be used against human beings, often in small ways but potentially scaling up to Westboro Baptist Church. And it's because of the latent violence at the heart of the Two Loves view that I think we must reject it as fundamentally mistaken. Because once you admit the possibility that the two loves exist, you admit the possibility that they can come into conflict. And with that possibility a Pandora's Box is opened. The existence of a Westboro Baptist Church becomes inevitable. All it takes is a Fred Phelps to push the conflict between the two loves to the extreme.

But in contrast to this Two Loves view is the One Love view, that there's only one love at work in the greatest commandments. In this view, Jesus isn't quoting Leviticus 19:18 to bring a second love alongside the love of God, he's quoting Leviticus 19:18 *to specify what loving God consists of.* Leviticus 19:18 *interprets* Deuteronomy 6:4-5—the two passages are woven together to make one point: loving human beings is loving God and loving God is loving human beings. Only one love is at work, with no daylight between these two objects of love. Consequently, there is no conflict between loving God and loving people. Love is always unified:

> Whoever claims to love God yet hates a brother or sister is a liar. For whoever does not love their brother and sister, whom they have seen, cannot love God, whom they have not seen. (1 John 4:20)

According to the One Love view, loving our neighbors is the *complete and full expression* of what it means to love God. In the words of Romans 13:10, "Love does no harm to a neighbor. Therefore love is the fulfillment of the law."

We need to contrast the Two Love and One Love approaches to Christianity because it helps make the point that when we see toxic examples of "spiritual warfare"—God being used to hurt people—the problem isn't with "spiritual warfare" but with something different and deeper, a fundamental confusion about the heart of Jesus' teaching regarding the Shema. Get that wrong and everything goes wrong, not just with spiritual warfare but everything else in your Christianity. The problem isn't with "spiritual warfare" but with a Two Loves view that creates a separation and potential antagonism between loving God and loving human beings. And that road is paved all the way to Westboro Baptist Church.

By contrast, there's no potential for abuse, no possibility for a Westboro Baptist Church, when spiritual warfare flows out of a One Love view of the Greatest Commandments. In the One Love view it would be heretical to claim that you could hurt another human being in the name of loving, pleasing, or obeying God. In the One Love view, it's just not possible for those loves to come into conflict. To love God, Jesus said, is to love your neighbor as yourself. Full stop. Everything about spiritual warfare flows out of that basic understanding.

So here at the start, as we build a theology of spiritual warfare, let's keep in front of us a regulating biblical image about what we mean by spiritual warfare. This will be a regulating and biblical image that defines exactly what we mean when we describe something as "satanic" or "demonic." And importantly, this image of the demonic can never be used to harm or hurt human beings.

The image to place at the center of our vision of spiritual warfare comes from the Gospels. This image will be our foundation, the cornerstone for any and all conversation about spiritual warfare. From the Gospel of Matthew:

> From that time on Jesus began to explain to his disciples that he must go to Jerusalem and suffer many things at the hands of the elders, the chief priests and the teachers of the law, and that he must be killed and on the third day be raised to life.
>
> Peter took him aside and began to rebuke him. "Never, Lord!" he said. "This shall never happen to you!"
>
> Jesus turned and said to Peter, "Get behind me, Satan! You are a stumbling block to me; you do not have in mind the concerns of God, but merely human concerns."
>
> Then Jesus said to his disciples, "Whoever wants to be my disciple must deny themselves and take up their cross and follow me." (Matthew 16:21-24)

Jesus' words to Peter are harsh. "Get behind me, Satan!" But let's reflect on what Peter was doing and why Jesus invoked the Devil. Jesus was explaining that he was heading toward the cross. Peter, confused and appalled, pulls Jesus to the side and tries to convince Jesus to take a different path. Jesus then wheels on Peter and describes what Peter is saying as "satan."

Let us recall, "satan" simply means "opponent," "adversary," or "accuser." Being a "satan" means being *against* something. So when Jesus calls Peter a satan what was Peter opposing?

Peter was opposing the *cross*. Peter was tempting Jesus, calling Jesus away from self-giving love. Facing this temptation, Jesus decisively pushes it behind him. Jesus says, "Get behind me, Satan!" and sets his face toward the cross.

And Jesus goes further. The way of the cross isn't just for Jesus. It's for every follower of Jesus. Everyone, Jesus says, must take up the cross to follow him.

And what this means, and this is the key point, is that every follower of Jesus faces this same choice, the choice Peter put before Jesus. The choice is between Satan and the cross. That's the fork in the road.

The satanic is everything which tempts us away from taking up our cross in following Jesus. This is critical for a theology of spiritual warfare, as the cross of Jesus is the quintessential expression of self-giving, self-donating, and sacrificial love. The satanic and the demonic are all those forces tempting us away from this love.

By spiritual warfare, I mean the choice between the cross and all that is tempting us away from the cross.

And by the satanic, I mean all that is *opposed* or *adversarial* to love, all that is opposed to the cross.

Allow me to use some theological jargon: our regulating image in Jesus' rebuke of Peter reveals the *cruciform* (cross-shaped) nature of spiritual warfare. We might say that spiritual warfare is the constant battle *to maintain this cruciform shape* in a world pushing a very different pattern upon us, a world trying to squeeze us into a very different sort of mold.

For example, a few weeks ago I was having a conversation with my youngest son Aidan, who is fifteen. I was trying to share with Aidan why showing kindness is so important in our world, why kindness needs to be intentionally cultivated and protected. I said to him, "Aidan, the world is cold and lonely and mean. Kindness is precious and rare. So practice it and cherish it." I shared that conversation with my Bible class and now that assessment—"the world is cold and lonely and mean"—has become a bit of a joke in our home and at church. And while my words might have been a bit overblown (and I beg for some forgiveness, as I was trying to get the attention of my teenage son), they are telling the truth about the world. The world *is* cold and lonely and mean. To live a cross-shaped and cruciform life in our world, a life committed to love and kindness, is a difficult thing. When I shared my "cold lonely and mean" speech with my mother-in-law Kathleen, she pointed me—Kathleen is an English teacher—to the final lines of Matthew Arnold's famous poem "Dover Beach":

> Ah, love, let us be true
> To one another! for the world, which seems
> To lie before us like a land of dreams,
> So various, so beautiful, so new,
> Hath really neither joy, nor love, nor light,
> Nor certitude, nor peace, nor help for pain;
> And we are here as on a darkling plain
> Swept with confused alarms of struggle and flight,
> Where ignorant armies clash by night.

That's spiritual warfare—being true to love in a world that hath neither joy, nor love, nor light, nor peace, nor hope for pain.

That's what I was trying to convey to my teenage son. The world is cold, lonely, and mean. Love is scarce, so be true to love.

In words of the great Pat Benatar, love is a battlefield.

That's spiritual warfare.

Chapter 10

The War of the Lamb

I VIVIDLY REMEMBER the day I started taking the Devil seriously. I was teaching class out at the prison. We were at the start of Matthew 5, the start of the Sermon on the Mount, the Beatitudes. I was reading through them. "Blessed are the poor in spirit. . . . Blessed are those that mourn. . . . Blessed are the meek."

But then I stopped.

I stopped because I'd noticed something on the faces of the men. Skepticism. Growing skepticism that culminated when I hit the word "meek." So I put my Bible down and looked around. "Looking at your faces," I said, "it doesn't seem like you're buying this." There was an awkward pause, a lot of staring at the ground and uncomfortable shifting in the seats. Finally one of the men spoke up.

"It's not that we disagree, but you just can't do that stuff in here. In here *meekness* is mistaken for *weakness*."

And the implication was clear. If you are weak you'll get hurt. Inside a maximum security prison, weakness is dangerous.

"You can't do that stuff in here." That comment shook me. And I struggled with how to respond. I was leaving in thirty minutes, so who was I to insist that these men become "weak" in such a dangerous place?

To this day, I vividly recall that Monday night out at the prison. That night was a turning point for me, a conversion experience. That was the night I witnessed a head-on spiritual collision: at close range saw the Beatitudes crash into the world. And it wasn't pretty.

Later, after I had sorted through the wreckage of my well-prepared Bible study, I realized that was the night I started believing in the Devil.

From the beginning of this book I've been describing "the satan" as the force or forces that are adversarial to love and the kingdom of God. And that night out at the prison I stood face to face with the Devil.

There were forces that were adversarial to meekness in the world of the prison, and to all of the Beatitudes, making the Way of Jesus risky, costly, and even dangerous. The Men in White wanted to follow Jesus, they wanted to obey, but they had their worries and fears. To follow Jesus was to swim upstream against a dark and satanic current.

"You can't do that stuff in here."

I didn't smell brimstone or see a horned shadow on the floor. But I do recall, in a way that haunts me to this day, love crashing into a wall. I was talking about Jesus and I'd run into something. And that something knocked me off my spiritual feet.

As I exited the prison, leaving the gates, gun turrets, and barbed wire behind me, I stood in the parking lot looking at the sunset. I was disturbed by what had happened in the class. After the comment, "You can't do that stuff in here," I was unable to move forward. I felt I had no authority to insist on the point. I'd preached the Beatitudes, the Men in White rejected them as impossible, and I'd let the matter drop. Who was I to demand that they follow Jesus in the world they were living in?

So I left disturbed, sad that the men locked up behind me lived in such a violent and brutal place, a place that made kindness and gentleness dangerous and risky. But I was also disturbed as I thought more about world I was entering, the world outside the prison. Are the Beatitudes, I stood in the parking lot wondering, any less crazy or risky in the world outside the prison? Hadn't I told my son Aidan that the world is cold, lonely, and mean? The world of the prison just takes that world to the extreme. But it's only a difference of degree. Meekness is taken for weakness everywhere in the world. The cross is always going to be deemed crazy, foolish, and insane in the eyes of the world. Love is risky and costly.

"You can't do that stuff in here."

"Or out here," I thought.

For the first time in my life the Beatitudes *frightened* me. Blessed are the meek? I saw the risk and danger. The same risk and danger Jesus' audience keenly felt, harassed and beleaguered as they were by oppressive colonial occupiers. Be meek in the face of imperial Rome? With crosses littering the landscape? You've got to be kidding me.

The first audience of the Beatitudes had the exact same incredulous reaction to Jesus that I'd just witnessed in the prison.

And standing in the parking lot that night it hit me like a ton of bricks. I whispered to myself, "You can't do that stuff anywhere." How many times have I turned my back on kindness, gentleness, and meekness? Following Jesus just doesn't seem like a good way to get ahead in the world. Best to look out for #1.

A Battle Fought for Love with Love

I think Pat Benatar got it right. Love is a battlefield. That's what I learned that night out at the prison. There are forces in the world satanically opposed to love. So if love is going to invade and establish a beachhead in our lives we're going to have to fight for it. That is what I mean by spiritual warfare. Just like Jesus, we have to say "Get behind me, Satan!" to follow Jesus to the cross.

But if spiritual warfare is a fight, it's a battle fought *with* love and *for* love.

For example, in the book of Revelation we read about a "war in heaven" where the armies of heaven do battle with Satan and his minions. True, the descriptions of this spiritual conflict in Revelation are gruesome and violent, reinforcing our worst fears about all this spiritual warfare talk. But that kneejerk assessment misses the heart of Revelation and its vision of what it means to wage a battle against the Devil with love.

That image of love as spiritual warfare in Revelation comes in chapters 4 and 5. In Revelation 4 John describes the throne room of heaven. A scroll is brought forward, the seals of which, when broken, bring about all the visions to follow. But John begins to weep with the hosts of heaven because no one is worthy to open the scroll and break the seals. John's lamentation is interrupted by an elder who says, "Do not weep! See, the Lion of the tribe of Judah, the Root of David, has triumphed. He is able to open the scroll and its seven seals."

This is a critical moment in the vision. The Lion of the tribe of Judah has triumphed! But when John turns to get a look at this conquering Lion he sees something strange and unexpected:

Then I saw a Lamb, looking as if it had been slain, standing at
the center of the throne.

Instead of a victorious, ferocious, and triumphant Lion sitting regally on Heaven's Throne John sees, strangely, a dead lamb. And yet, heaven breaks out in praise of the Lamb:

Worthy is the Lamb, who was slain,
to receive power and wealth and wisdom and strength
and honor and glory and praise! (Revelation 5:12)

Christ's victory over Satan is won through sacrificial love. The Lion triumphs in battle *as the Lamb.*

And in its own battle with Satan the church militant uses the same weapon—the blood of the Lamb, sacrificial love. From Revelation 12:

Then war broke out in heaven. . . . The great dragon was hurled down—that ancient serpent called the devil, or Satan, who leads the whole world astray . . .

Then I heard a loud voice in heaven say:

"They triumphed over him
by the blood of the Lamb
and by the word of their testimony;
they did not love their lives so much
as to shrink from death . . ."

Noteworthy in this description of the church in Revelation 12 is how the followers of Jesus do not take lives but give their own lives up as martyrs. The War of the Lamb—the battle for love fought with love—is a battle fought by soldiers who are willing to have their blood shed rather than shed the blood of their enemies.

Outside of the Gospels and Revelation we also see the love-is-a-battlefield metaphor used in Colossians 2:15 where, once again, explicit military imagery is used to describe the triumph of Jesus's love on the cross:

And having disarmed the powers and authorities, he made a public spectacle of them, triumphing over them by the cross.

The phrase "public spectacle" refers to the victory parade of a conquering Caesar or King who, in returning to the capital after a great military victory, would publicly display on a victory march the spoils and prisoners of war before a cheering and adoring citizenry. It's a striking image of military conquest and victory. But shockingly and subversively the writer of Colossians suggests that *on the cross Jesus is leading just such a victory parade!* That is a mind-blowing assertion, that the sacrificial love Jesus displayed on the cross disarmed the "powers and authorities" and made "a public spectacle of them." That is the War of the Lamb, a military victory won for love with love. That is how the battle against Satan is won. The war in heaven against the dragon described in Revelation is the same battle we fight on earth. Minute by minute. Day by day. The path toward sacrificial love lies before us. Will we conquer the dragon with the blood of the Lamb? Will we say resolutely "Get behind me, Satan!" and follow Jesus to the cross?

Since that night when I first taught the Beatitudes out at the prison I've had many, many more conversations with the Men in White about what it means to follow Jesus in the world. The Men in White have shared story after story about their daily battles to follow Jesus, their heroic struggles to create a beachhead of love within the prison. And they do succeed. Here and there they experience the kingdom come on earth as it is in heaven. But the price can be costly. Last week Cody shared with me what happened to Billy. Billy was in a prison gang but he converted to Christianity. So Billy wanted out. You're beaten to get into the gang and you're beaten if you want to leave. They beat Billy so hard, Cody said, that Billy's eyeball popped out, still attached to the nerves. They had to push Billy's eye back into its socket.

Love is a battlefield.

That's a pretty heroic story, what Billy endured to follow Jesus. But in a world satanically opposed to love, love is always going to involve some battlefield heroics. Maybe for you and me love doesn't involve the risk of being beaten. But we are called to display bravery in other ways. For example, maybe love means you have to give up some vision of worldly success. The War of the Lamb—the sacrificial love of Jesus—might not come with a physical cost but it often comes with a *social* cost. A loss of reputation or social advancement. As Paul noted in 1 Corinthians 1:18, the cross is foolishness to the world. The War of the Lamb is loving in ways that look silly, stupid, and absurd to those observing the decisions we make. A few years ago I spoke at a church and a few months later I received this email:

Dr. Beck,
There's absolutely no way you remember this, but about 11 months ago you spoke at our church and my wife and I came up to say hello after church.

At the time I was the Director of Education at a prestigious intuition. I'm not bragging about that, but what you said at our church upper-cutted me in my heart. I realized that Sunday that my career was about me. My career wasn't about my wife or God, or anything but myself.

So last August my family moved and I started teaching World History to 10th Graders in an inner-city high school where 98% of the students are on free & reduced lunch. Two weekends ago my wife and I went to the hospital with a box of diapers to visit a 16-year-old student who had just had a baby. I have four other pregnant students, a male student who is 16 and has two kids, and a student who just got arrested for assault. I have never worked as hard in my life as I am now. There are days where I work harder than I did in a month at my other job, but I've never felt more alive, and we truly feel like this is a mission field.

I just wanted you to know that a sermon you preached at church with a parking lot full of SUVs actually changed my life, my wife's life, our daughter's life, and—ideally—152 10th graders' lives.

Living out the Beatitudes in a maximum-security prison? Getting jumped so bad by a gang that your eyeball is knocked out of its socket? Giving up a prestigious position to teach history in an inner-city school? That's the foolishness of the cross. But that is how the battle with Satan is fought and won. A battle fought for love with love.

That is the War of the Lamb.

Chapter 11

Angels and Demons

THE DEVIL IS boring.

That was the assessment of Hannah Arendt after she had looked evil in the eye. Evil is banal. Evil is ordinary, common, trivial, shallow, superficial, and uninteresting. Evil is a yawner.

"The banality of evil" is what Arendt saw when she looked into the heart and mind of Nazi war criminal Adolf Eichmann.

Eichmann was called "The Architect of the Holocaust" because during World War II he was the SS officer charged with handling the logistics of the mass deportation of the Jewish population to the ghettos and, eventually, to the extermination camps. Eichmann was, in essence, the Bureaucrat of the Holocaust. He was the Office Manager and the Paper-Pusher of Death.

After the war, most of the surviving Nazi war criminals were rounded up and put on trial at Nuremberg, but not Eichmann. He escaped and found his way to Argentina, and there he lived under a false identity for many years.

Eichmann's true identity was eventually uncovered, and on May 11, 1960 he was captured by Israeli operatives and taken to Israel to stand trial for crimes against humanity and the Jewish people.

The Eichmann trial became an international sensation as the whole world watched the first televised courtroom trial in history. At the end of the internationally televised trial, Eichmann was found guilty on all counts and was sentenced to death. He was executed on May 31, 1962.

Hannah Arendt was a political philosopher who, because she was Jewish, had fled Germany during Hitler's rise to power. She'd missed an opportunity to cover the Nuremburg war crimes trials, but she didn't want to miss the Eichmann trial. She convinced the *New Yorker* to send her to Jerusalem to cover the trial, giving Arendt what she wanted most: her own personal, face-to-face confrontation with the Devil.

For both personal and professional reasons, Arendt wanted to see a Nazi war criminal up close and in the flesh. She wanted to look into the eyes of evil. Arendt came to Jerusalem looking for the Monster.

But what Arendt found in Eichmann was something quite different. Eichmann was bland, polite, and intellectually shallow. By the end of the trial Arendt concluded that Eichmann was more of a fool than a devil. Arendt wrote in her account of the trial, *Eichmann in Jerusalem*, "Everybody could see that this man was not a 'monster,' but it was difficult indeed not to suspect that he was a clown."[1]

Arendt wanted to know why Eichmann participated in the Holocaust. But the answer she got wasn't what she expected. Eichmann did what he did because he loved his country, because he trusted his superiors, because he never questioned their orders, because he went to work each day and did his job. He was a small cog in a much larger machine, not one to speak up to power.

---

1. Hannah Arendt, *Eichmann in Jerusalem: A Report on the Banality of Evil*, revised and enlarged edition (New York: Viking, 1964), 54.

Arendt coined the term "the banality of evil" to describe Eichmann's self-defense, a defense rooted in an unthinking patriotism, deference to authority, and focus on just doing his job. We often assume that evil is some dark, spooky, occult force, like the demon possession in *The Exorcist*. But after seeing Eichmann, Arendt was convinced that the face of evil in the world is actually quite ordinary and boring. Evil is as boring as forwarding emails and making copies at the office. Evil is keeping the paperwork moving.

Evil, according to Arendt, is unthinking assent to the values, norms, and expectations of our world and the institutions we work and serve within, informal and formal, large and small. Evil is unthinking conformity to the *Zeitgeist*, a German word that means "the spirit of the age." Eichmann submitted to the Zeitgeist of Nazi Germany, as did so many others. That's what we mean when we say someone "drank the Kool Aid," a reference to the mass suicide of Jim Jones's cult members who killed themselves on Jones's orders by drinking Kool Aid laced with cyanide. The followers of Jones did not question the Zeitgeist of the cult. Eichmann didn't question the Zeitgeist of Germany. And we fail to question the Zeitgeist of our own time and place.

Testing the Zeitgeist

In 1 John 4:1 we are admonished: "Beloved, do not believe every spirit, but test the spirits to see whether they are from God." Test the spirits? When you're a doubting and disenchanted Christian the imperative to test or discern the spirits is confusing and weird. And a bit spooky. But the story of Eichmann helps us here.

Discerning the spirits in the world at work within cultures, systems, nations, and institutions—spiritually assessing how we might be "drinking the Kool Aid"—involves determining if the spirit, Zeitgeist, culture, value system, way-of-life, or ideology at work is satanically adversarial to the cross. Discerning the spirits is testing to see if the Zeitgeists we encounter in any given context are pro-Jesus or anti-Jesus. Because when we fail to tests the spirits we become accomplices, like an Eichmann, of the anti-Jesus forces at work in the world. And we aid and abet without any malice or forethought. Because we really haven't given it any thought at all. We've just drunk the Kool Aid.

Doubting and disenchanted Christians need to recover a way of speaking about angels and demons because the language of discerning the spirits helps us shift focus away from concrete examples of oppression *to attend to the Zeitgeist that produces these injustices.* You can't understand Auschwitz until you understand the Zeitgeist that produced the concentration camps and how that Zeitgeist made genocide seem like just another day at the office—and how that Zeitgeist *hid* and *normalized* the evil.

We can think of similar examples affecting us today. I recently took a bus trip with twenty preachers from my faith tradition through historic locations in the American civil rights struggle in Montgomery, Selma, and Birmingham. Ten of the preachers were black and ten were white, and we took the trip to talk about race relations in our churches and in the nation. One of the things we spoke about is how the struggle for racial justice has changed since the 1960s. During the Montgomery Bus Boycott, the sit-in movement, the Freedom rides, and Freedom Summer, direct-action campaigns were aimed at concrete and visible locations of Jim Crow segregation. From segregated seating on buses to obstacles to voter registration. And with the passage of the Civil Rights and Voting Rights Acts in '64 and '65 these overt locations of injustice were removed from American society. Apartheid officially ended in America. And yet, America continues to be a highly segregated society and racial injustices persist. From police shootings to poverty to mass incarceration to the quality of schools, we are awash in the sad statistics that reveal the racial injustices still plaguing America. But with the official ending of apartheid in America, where, today, are we to find the sources of these injustices? To be sure, there is still much work to be done on the policy front to make our society fairer and more just. Caring as

I do about the criminal justice system in America, there are many things still to fix, from mandatory sentencing to capital punishment, to say nothing about how the rich have access to quality legal representation in a way the poor do not.

However, as we rode through the South, those twenty preachers and I suspected that these policy fixes were only small tweaks in what was a larger, more spiritual problem—a problem with the American Zeitgeist. As one of the black preachers said, "It's not the laws that are the problem, but the unfair *implementation* of the laws." For example, stop-and-frisk laws are not, as they sit on the books, inherently racist. The problem comes when those laws are *applied* unfairly, used mainly against African Americans, sweeping greater numbers of them into the criminal justice system. Today we don't mainly detect systemic racism by examining *written* laws and policies. Today we detect racism by *outcomes*, in things like poverty or incarceration statistics. Something is happening between *policy* and *outcome*.

According to the preachers on the bus, it's the Zeitgeist. On the books, apartheid may have ended in America, but we are still plagued by a spirit of racism. Racism is what causes policies to be implemented in a biased way. But racism isn't a law or policy. Racism is a Zeitgeist, a spirit, an anti-Jesus force at work in the world.

Which puts the political activist in a bit of a pickle. March and protest all you want, but racism, as a spirit, can't be fixed by passing laws. Political activism is largely impotent in addressing the spiritual problems facing America and the world. A new president or a new Congress isn't going to heal what ails us. If the Zeitgeist is the problem, then the battle is no longer merely political. The battle is inherently *spiritual* in nature.

For example, during our bus trip the twenty preachers and I spent time with Fred Grey, who was the lawyer for Rosa Parks and Martin Luther King during the Montgomery Bus Boycott. Outside of Thurgood Marshall, Grey is the most significant civil rights lawyer in American history, the lawyer who filed seminal school integration lawsuits and who represented the victims of the infamous Tuskegee Syphilis Study. During our time with Brother Grey, he said something that gets to the distinction between the spiritual and the political and our stubborn lack of racial progress since the '60s.

"I was able to change the laws," he said, "but I couldn't change the hearts."

Again, doubting and disenchanted Christians often adopt a Scooby-Dooification approach when it comes to spiritual warfare, reducing spiritual warfare to political activism. But when Christians do this they miss what is perhaps the most critical piece of the puzzle. As Fred Grey put it, they miss the *hearts*. They miss the *Zeitgeist*, the *spirit* of the age. They miss the *spiritual* aspect of spiritual warfare.

And before you can *resist* the Zeitgeist, through confession and repentance, we have to *discern* the spirits of the age. And this is where the language of angels and demons can be helpful.

Recall how in the Bible the political and the spiritual are tightly associated and hard to disentangle. Rather than a scene from *The Exorcist*, when the ancients thought of angels and demons they also thought of things like "thrones" and political "dominions." "Demonic strongholds" were locations of *political* power. To be sure, the ancients believed in demon possession, but when they spoke of a battle against the principalities and powers—spiritual forces of wickedness in high places—they were also thinking of City Hall.

Tugging on the Demon Thread

But in our focus upon political injustice we often fail to reckon with the *spirituality* at work within systems, structures, and institutions; we fail to test their animating Zeitgeist. Recovering the biblical language of angels and demons can help us with this by focusing our attention upon how our hearts and minds become captured, numbed, distracted, and even "possessed" by the dark spiritualities at work in the world. Learning to discern the spirits offers us a way forward when a purely political vision of spiritual warfare proves impotent, when *hearts* rather than *laws* have to change.

I do realize that doubting and disenchanted Christians are going to balk at speaking about angels and demons and the discerning of spirits. So to help with this, to illustrate the connection between angels, demons, and the principalities and powers, let's trace an angelic and demonic thread through the Bible, starting in the Old Testament and going all the way through to the Book of Revelation.

The thread starts in the Old Testament. We generally assume that the Old Testament writers and the ancient Hebrews were monotheists, believing in only one God, and that the "gods" of other nations didn't exist. Idols created to worship foreign "gods" were mere wood and stone. There was nothing spiritual or spooky behind these idols. Other gods simply weren't real. There are many passages in the Old Testament that express this strictly monotheistic worldview, where one God and only this one God exists in the heavenly realm. Consider these lines from Psalm 115:

> Why do the nations say,
> "Where is their God?"
> Our God is in heaven;
> he does whatever pleases him.
> But their idols are silver and gold,
> made by human hands.
> They have mouths, but cannot speak,
> eyes, but cannot see.
> They have ears, but cannot hear,
> noses, but cannot smell.
> They have hands, but cannot feel,
> feet, but cannot walk,
> nor can they utter a sound with their throats.

We can also think here of stories like the contest in 1 Kings between Elijah and the prophets of Baal on Mount Carmel. God acts in vindication of Elijah, sending fire. Baal does nothing because Baal doesn't exist.

But there are many other stories in the Old Testament where heaven seems filled with angelic and godlike beings. The opening scene in Job is a good example: "One day the angels [literally, the sons of God] came to present themselves before the Lord, and Satan also came with them." In these texts the heavens are crowded. God doesn't seem to be all alone. God is portrayed not as the *only* God but as the *Supreme* God, the ruler over all the other lesser gods who were worshiped by the nations.

These lesser, *rival gods* were associated with *rival nations* and how the worship of God in Israel created a contrast with these political and spiritual powers. A contrast of rival political and spiritual *kingdoms*.

Beyond the spiritual critique of idolatry—Hey, you're worshiping the wrong god!—Israel's criticism of these rival gods and their kingdoms was also political in nature. Specifically, these rival gods were the source of oppression and injustice in the world. What we see in Psalm 82, for example, is a vision of "the heavenly realm" where "the sons of god" are identified as regional and national deities tasked with governing the affairs of earth. You catch another glimpse of this very early in the Old Testament in Deuteronomy 32:8-9:

> When the Most High gave to the nations their inheritance,
> when he divided mankind,
> he fixed the borders of the peoples
> according to the number of the sons of God.
> But the Lord's portion is his people,
> Jacob his allotted heritage.[2]

When God divided up the nations each nation was given to a "son of God," and in Psalm 82 God convenes a Divine Council of these gods. This Divine Council is sort of a boardroom meeting among

---

2. ESV.

the gods, with God running the meeting as the chairman of the board. God has some harsh things to say to the gods running the kingdoms of the world: the gods of the nations aren't doing a very good job; they're allowing violence and injustice to run wild in the streets. So God, CEO and chairman, tells the gods of the nations that they had better shape up or they will get fired from their jobs:

> God has taken his place in the divine council;
> in the midst of the gods he holds judgment:
> "How long will you judge unjustly
> and show partiality to the wicked?
> Give justice to the weak and the fatherless;
> maintain the right of the afflicted and the destitute.
> Rescue the weak and the needy;
> deliver them from the hand of the wicked."
> They have neither knowledge nor understanding,
> they walk about in darkness;
> all the foundations of the earth are shaken.
> I said, "You are gods,
> sons of the Most High, all of you;
> nevertheless, like men you shall die,
> and fall like any prince."[3]

God is going to destroy these gods because they're agents of oppression. These gods judge unjustly, they show partiality to the wicked. So God calls these gods to repentance, demanding that they give justice to the weak and the fatherless, that they maintain the rights of the afflicted and the destitute and that they rescue the weak and the needy from the hand of the wicked.

Notice in Psalm 82 how *the spirituality of the nation*—the god of the nation—is connected to *the political oppression* being experienced within that nation. Also note how *spiritual allegiance and obedience* to God brings *justice* and relief to those being oppressed.

---

3. ESV.

The reign of God on earth is thus both political and spiritual, involving the worship of God and the restoration of justice. In the biblical imagination the *worship* of God and *justice* are two sides of the same coin.

For example, consider the primal story of liberation in the Bible, the story of the Exodus. When we think of Moses confronting Pharaoh—who was considered to be one of those sons of god, the regional deity governing the political affairs of Egypt—we think of the words "Let my people go!" That is the cry of slaves. It is a cry for political emancipation and liberation.

But when we read the story of the Exodus this cry isn't initially a cry for *political* freedom, let my people go free from *slavery*. It is, rather, initially a cry of *spiritual* resistance, the demand to be free to *worship*. In his very first exchange with Pharaoh, this is what Moses requests (emphasis added):

> Afterward Moses and Aaron went to Pharaoh and said, "This is what the Lord, the God of Israel, says: 'Let my people go, *so that they may hold a festival to me in the wilderness.*'" (Exodus 5:1)

Moses' first request is simply *a request to worship God*. Before anything else the cry of liberation "Let my people go!" is an expression of *spiritual resistance*. It is a cry for emancipation from the ruling gods, the oppressive spiritual Zeitgeist of Egypt. This is the same spiritual revolt we see in Daniel as he continues to pray in Babylon, and in Shadrach, Meshach, and Abednego when they refuse to worship Nebuchadnezzar's idol.

Of course we know how the story continues. Pharaoh rejects Moses' request, believing that the Hebrews are simply being lazy. Pharaoh then becomes even more oppressive, demanding more bricks with less straw.

Notice in the Exodus story how *rejecting the worship of God* is connected to political *oppression*. Instead of submitting to God, Pharaoh increases oppression and injustice in the land. Just like we see in Psalm 82.

All through the Bible a failure to show spiritual allegiance to God goes hand in hand with political oppression. This highlights how spiritual warfare can be described as *a battle between rival spiritual allegiances*, allegiances that bring either peace or oppression to earth.

The connection between spiritual powers and political institutions is picked up in the book of Daniel, and here we see a development with the regional *gods* of the nations now described as territorial *demons*. In Daniel 10:3 the angel Gabriel reports being delayed by a regional spirit described as the "prince of Persia," the ruling demon of Babylon. The archangel Michael comes to Gabriel's rescue, a foreshadowing of Revelation's "war in heaven" between Michael and the Dragon. It's a fascinating text, this clash of angels and demons, but notice something we tend to miss. The demon that Gabriel and Michael are tangling with is associated with a *political power*—the nation of Babylon.

That diabolical connection—demons associated with the political kingdoms of the world—is highlighted right at the start of the New Testament. In the temptation narratives in the Gospels, Satan is described as ruler over all the kingdoms in the world:

> The devil led him up to a high place and showed him in an instant all the kingdoms of the world. And he said to him, "I will give you all their authority and splendor; it has been given to me, and I can give it to anyone I want to." (Luke 4:5-6)

I don't think the connection between the spiritual and the political could be any clearer. The price for political power is spiritual allegiance.

Jesus rejects both offers, refusing to worship Satan and refusing to rule the world through political power. Turning his back on Satan, Jesus sets out to establish a very different sort of kingdom exercising a very different sort of power as a very different sort of King.

This image of Satan as the spiritual power behind the kingdoms of the world is also observed in the Book of Revelation. In Revelation we are given the image of the city of Babylon. Spiritually speaking, Babylon is blasphemous and idolatrous. Babylon is demon-haunted. But Babylon is also described as *the political power that rules the whole world*. As it says in Revelation 17:19, Babylon is "the great city that rules over the kings of the earth." Spiritually and politically, as servant of the Beast, Babylon represents the spiritual and political forces in the world waging war against the Lamb and the kingdom of God. And as the vision unfolds Babylon is brought under judgment, the judgment of Psalm 82 that God brings against oppressive nations.

The oppressive and exploitative aspects of Babylon are highlighted by who mourns for Babylon when she falls. Who weeps for Babylon? The *kings* and the *merchants* because they "grew rich" from Babylon's economic and political exploitation of the world (Revelation 18:3, 11-13).

Spiritual warfare, then, is for the people of God to "come out" from Babylon, the *demon-haunted* and *oppressive* city (Revelation 18:1-4).

Demon Possession and Guardian Angels

I've now tugged on the demonic thread that runs through Scripture, pointing out how our struggle with the principalities and powers is both political and spiritual in nature, how a demonic Zeitgeist sits behind injustice and oppression. The image of Babylon in Revelation, the *demon-haunted* and *violent* city, makes the connection crystal clear. When we speak of "demonic strongholds" in the world Babylon should come to mind, locations of spiritual darkness in the world where human beings are being exploited.

So we see a connection in the Bible between *demonic Zeitgeist* and *injustice*. But let's dig a little deeper here and make all this a little more practical and personal, because the specter of Adolf Eichmann continues to haunt us. It's one thing to say that demonic Zeitgeists are at work within oppressive political systems, but it's another and harder thing to come to grips with how *I* am blinded, like Eichmann was blinded, to the Zeitgeists of my own time and place. We need to test and discern the spirits in our own contexts and in our own hearts and minds.

According to Walter Wink, one of the problems many modern Christians have with how the Bible talks about angels, demons, and other spiritual forces in the heavenly realm is the Up/Down metaphor used by the ancients in relating the heavenly and spiritual to the earthy and physical.[4] The ancients saw heaven and the spiritual realm as existing "above" the earth. God and the angels lived in the heavens overhead and looked down upon the earth. The spiritual realm existed above the physical. And this ancient understanding—the heavens existing *above* the earth—can be a stumbling point for doubting and disenchanted Christians. In an era of space exploration we know that there is no heaven above us. Heaven isn't a city sitting on a cloud. And if heaven isn't located above us, it seems like space exploration has banished the spiritual realm from the universe.[5]

So while the ancients might have thought that the powers were literally overhead we treat that language as metaphorical. Where, then, are we to locate these powers? Wink suggests that when we refer to the spiritual or heavenly realm, we trade the ancient Up/Down metaphor for an Inside/Outside metaphor. Rather than the spiritual being *up* and the physical being *down*, the spiritual is the *inside* and the physical is the *outside*. This suggestion is attractive for a couple of different reasons.

First, the Inside/Outside metaphor holds together another metaphor we use for the spiritual versus physical distinction. Specifically, the spiritual is typically associated with the realm that is "unseen"

---

4. See Wink's Powers trilogy: *Naming the Powers* (1984), *Unmasking the Powers* (1986), and *Engaging the Powers* (1992).

5. Modern Christians shouldn't get too smug and dismissive about all this. Just think of how we talk about spiritual matters (God *watches over* us), legal matters (the Supreme Court is the *highest court*), and economic matters (the *upper* and *lower* classes). So maybe we should cut the Bible some slack on the up/down, above/below language.

and the physical with that which is "seen." The Inside/Outside metaphor works well with this unseen/spiritual versus seen/physical distinction. For example, when I look at you I see your physical being. But what is happening on the *inside*? What do you love? Fear? Care about? What are your deepest motivations? What drives you? Such questions are exploring what is going on "inside" of you, the realm of the psyche. And *psyche*, we know, even in the Bible, is the Greek word for "soul." The *inside* of you, the *unseen* part of you, is the *spiritual* side of you.

And the same goes for organizations, institutions, nations, or any other social arrangement. Inside any social organization—big or small, formal or informal—are values, norms, habits, beliefs, procedures, customs, cultures, worldviews, expectations, rules, ideologies, and practices that come together to create the "spirit" that holds the organization together, the Zeitgeist. Every organization or institution has an Outside and an Inside. And while our conversation about Zeitgeists in this chapter has mainly been about nation-states, *every* organization and group has a Zeitgeist, an inner spiritual climate that affects those within the institution. This helps make the point more personal and practical. Because every family has a Zeitgeist. Every place of work. Every church. Even social media have a Zeitgeist.

This helps us understand why, in chapters 2 and 3 in the book of Revelation, Jesus addresses the *angel* of each of the seven churches. In addressing the angel of each church, we see how Jesus is discerning and testing the *spirits* of the seven churches, the good, the bad, and the ugly of the spiritual Zeitgeist at work in each church.

Think of all places you've worked in your life. Each workplace had a spiritual atmosphere or climate that affected you. That climate affected your mood, your health, your choices, your way of seeing yourself, and your view of the world. Sometimes that climate was healthy and life-giving, other times it was soul-crushing and dehumanizing.

Discerning the spirits is attending to the spiritual climate— the angel, the Zeitgeist—at work in each of these places, and most especially, discerning how the spirituality of an environment has infiltrated our hearts and minds. And if you'd like to call that demon possession, I'll go along with that. I think that's a good description of what happened to Adolf Eichmann. He was possessed by the dark angel of Nazism when he followed Hitler's orders.

By contrast, when spiritual climates are healthy and life-giving we could call those climates *angelic*, naming them as locations of grace and peace where the kingdom is experienced on earth as it is heaven. Locations where God is worshiped and Jesus reigns. We experience life in these places as their angelic spirit cares for and protects us. Outposts of the kingdom become our guardian angels.

The Power of the Air

In Ephesians 2:2 the "ways of the world" are described as being controlled by the Devil who is "the prince of the power of the air." And air, we know, is everywhere but invisible.

The Zeitgeist is the spiritual air we breathe but rarely notice because we can't even see it. It's like that story about the two young fish swimming together. An older fish swims past them and says, "Morning boys! How's the water?" Puzzled, the two young fish look at each other and say, "What the hell is water?"

The Zeitgeist of an organization, institution, culture, or nation is like the air or water: the unseen spiritual force guiding everything, but so hidden, so normal, and so obvious that no one notices it, let alone questions or dissents. Who notices the air or water? That's what causes the banality of evil. That's what makes the Devil so boring.

No one *discerns* the spirits because no one *sees* the spirits.

And that's why we need to talk more about angels and demons. We need to name the unseen forces. We need to recognize the power of the air.

Chapter 12

Resist the Devil

GONORRHEA ON VALENTINE'S Day.

I don't know about you, but that has my vote for the best lyric in all of contemporary Christian music.

If you surf online for "greatest" or "most influential" albums of all time in contemporary Christian music, Larry Norman's 1972 release *Only Visiting This Planet* is often found at or near the top of the list. An influential album among the Jesus People movement that fused hippie culture with evangelical Christianity in the '70s, many of the songs on *Only Visiting This Planet* spoke directly to the youth culture that emerged out of the Summer of Love ('67) and Woodstock ('69). The excesses of those years, sexually and chemically, were beginning to leave their mark. Jimi Hendrix and Janis Joplin died of overdoses in 1970. Jim Morrison died of an overdose a year later in '71. By the early '70s the Age of Aquarius was losing its shine.

In the song "Why Don't You Look into Jesus" from *Only Visiting This Planet*, Norman speaks an evangelistic message into the darkness and disillusionment that many were experiencing at the time:

Sipping whiskey from a paper cup,
You drown your sorrows till you can't stand up.
Take a look at what you've done to yourself,
Why don't you put the bottle back on the shelf?
Yellow fingers from your cigarettes,
Your hands are shaking while your body sweats.
Why don't you look into Jesus, He's got the answer.

Gonorrhea on Valentine's Day,
And you're still looking for the perfect lay.
You think rock and roll will set you free,
You'll be dead before you're thirty-three.
Shooting junk till you're half insane,
Broken needle in your purple vein.
Why don't you look into Jesus, He's got the answer.

At Freedom Fellowship we struggle with addictions and sexual hurts of various sorts. So recently when it was my turn to teach at Freedom, I played "Why Don't You Look into Jesus." It's a funky song and I knew we'd have a great discussion about it.

And with lyrics like "Gonorrhea on Valentine's Day," we had a lot to talk about. We all identified with the disillusionment expressed in the song. We shared honest stories that night about addiction, recovery, and relapse. We shared stories about our sexual lives, stories of abuse, betrayal, emptiness, exploitation, and abandonment, about how we had hoped that sex was leading us to Valentine's Day, but how we ended up with something else, something emotionally sad, lonely, and painful.

And while we shared a lot of sad stories that night at Freedom, we also shared stories of recovery, hope, love, restoration, and resurrection. In Jesus our sad stories found the Valentine's Day we'd all been looking for.

As I've said, we talk a lot about Satan and demons at Freedom. And more often than not when we're talking about the Devil we're talking about things like addiction. We talk about similar things out at the prison. When the Men in White and I talk about "resisting the devil," we talk about drug use, pornography, and violence.

I was visiting with Corey before the Bible study a few weeks ago. Corey was sharing how hard it was to follow Jesus in the prison. "Pornography and drugs are everywhere!" Corey said. "Everywhere you turn it's in your face. Just the other day my cellmate, who knows I'm trying to stay away from drugs, comes walking into our cell and offers me a hit on a joint he's smoking. And I said, 'Get that the fuck away from me! You know I'm trying to stay away from that shit!'"

Resisting the devil? *"Get that the fuck away from me!"* That's often what it looks like.

Pizza Jesus, with Sauce and Cheese Please

Addiction. Lust. Violence. When we're talking about the Devil out at the prison or at Freedom, these are the things we're mostly talking about, things we'd describe as sin.

But here's the weird thing. A lot of Christians are embarrassed by sin. We don't want to talk about it. Especially when it comes to sex.

You see this embarrassment a lot among Christians who are post-evangelical or post-fundamentalist, Christians who were raised in puritanical churches where sin, holiness, purity, piety, and personal morality were talked about all the time in ways that created loads of guilt, fear, and shame. I understand. Growing up in a conservative church I knew that being a "good person" meant avoiding drugs and sex. And coming out of pietistic churches like this we want to avoid talking about sin because talking about sin makes you sound like a judgmental and holier-than-thou Christian who's obsessed with sex.

The other hesitancy to talk about personal morality has to do with how we need to address *systemic* evils—social injustice and oppression. By focusing so much on this struggle we can come to wholly ignore the *personal* and *moral* aspects of the Christian walk. We talk a lot about *justice*, but we have almost nothing to say about *holiness*.

Following the lead of Thomas Jefferson, doubting and disenchanted Christians snip the supernatural stuff out of their picture of Jesus, his battle with Satan in particular. And if you're too embarrassed to talk about sin you're snipping all the moral stuff out of Jesus as well. And with the spiritual and moral stuff snipped out of Jesus, there's not much Jesus left over. Thomas Jefferson's snipping might have been radical, but at least he left in the moral stuff, something doubting and disenchanted Christians seem unwilling to do, embarrassed as they are about sin. If you came over to my house for pizza and I left off the sauce and cheese, giving you only a plain crust, you'd likely argue I wasn't serving you pizza. Same goes for Jesus. Minus the moral and spiritual parts, the Jesus of doubting and disenchanted Christians isn't really Jesus anymore. He's pizza without the sauce and cheese.

Taking It Personally

Holiness is one of the things that gets lost when we stop talking about the Devil. We miss how spiritual warfare is often a personal, private, and intimate battle against our own inner demons.

Spiritual warfare isn't just about a political struggle with the principalities and powers. Spiritual warfare is also about sin and morality. Over and over spiritual warfare is described in the Bible as a personal and moral struggle to resist the Devil:

> Submit yourselves, then, to God. Resist the devil, and he will flee from you. (James 4:7)

> Be alert and of sober mind. Your enemy the devil prowls around like a roaring lion looking for someone to devour. (1 Peter 5:8)

> Put on the full armor of God, so that you can take your stand against the devil's schemes . . . take up the shield of faith, with

which you can extinguish all the flaming arrows of the evil one.
(Ephesians 6:11, 16)

A theology of spiritual warfare should speak to all the ways that we, personally, come under spiritual attack, and how we, personally, work to resist the Devil in our own hearts and minds.

If Satan is anything in the Bible, he's a tempter. We think of Eve being tempted by the serpent in the Garden of Eden, Satan bringing tragedy upon Job to test his faith, and Jesus being tempted by Satan in the wilderness. Looking over these stories, I think that we experience personal opposition from Satan in two different ways.

When we look at Eve in the Garden of Eden and Jesus in the wilderness we observe how Satan is associated with the *temptation to sin*. The way of the kingdom lies before us and Satan is tempting us away from that path. Temptation is what Corey was experiencing when his cellmate walked in offering him drugs. To stay clean Corey had to resist the Devil. And this is something we all do every day. Even atheists have to say no to personal temptations that draw them away from some vision of goodness they want for themselves and the world. The personal journey toward goodness, wholeness, and peace is difficult. Just like Eve and Jesus, we are tempted to get off-track.

The Unholy Divide

But while this seems obvious, many Christians remain reluctant to talk about sin, especially when it comes to failures of conventional Christian piety. For many conservative Christians, being a "good" person means displaying the virtues traditionally associated with puritanism and the Protestant work ethic, virtues like self-control, chastity, duty, diligence, fortitude, thrift, and self-reliance. And the focus is often on controlling physical appetites and cravings, resisting the lusts of the flesh. Growing up in my conservative church, being a "good" kid meant not having sex before marriage and not drinking, smoking, or doing drugs. But really, sex was the big thing. Avoid sex and you were successfully resisting the devil.

One of the reasons post-evangelical and post-fundamentalist Christians struggle with talking about sin is because we want to distance ourselves from that puritanical focus, especially when it comes to sex. But in our desire to avoid looking puritanical, we just clam up about sin and holiness. And without a moral aspect, faith is reduced to politics—Christianity becomes about voting well every four years.

For some reason—I blame the Devil—we've separated the moral and the political. Conservatives gets the moral and progressives get the political, each group acting as if the two things aren't intimately related. But can we really talk about the root causes of sex trafficking, pornography, and sexual abuse without having a conversation about lust? Can we really talk about poverty without a conversation about greed, consumerism, and materialism? Can we have a conversation about violence without a conversation about prejudice and hate?

The moral and the political are two sides of the same coin, each affecting the other. Moral failures—like greed or lust or prejudice—create unjust and oppressive political systems. And unjust political systems cause moral failures, throwing up steep obstacles in front of those seeking a better life for themselves and their loved ones. Scientists call this *reciprocal* causation. When it comes to the moral and the political it's not a simple A causes B or B causes A. The causation is back and forth: A causes B *and* B causes A. It's a feedback loop. I think this is one of the great failures of contemporary Christianity, how conservatives and progressives have divided up the moral and the political, effectively killing their ability address the gnarly realities facing us. Seriously, I blame the Devil. The great trick the Devil is playing on the church is the moral/political split that separates progressive and conservative Christians. Divide and conquer. The Devil asked conservative and progressive Christians to split the baby. And we did.

We need to overcome this divide. We need to talk more about resisting the Devil in ways that embrace both the political and the moral. We need to speak about morality in a way that avoids the puritanical, holier-than-thou trap.

The Moral Is the Political

We can do this if read the Bible more closely. For example, let's look closely at the context of James 4:7 where we're encouraged to "resist the devil."

For most of my life I took this command to be referring to things like lustful thoughts. Sure, lust is a problem that needs to be dealt with, but if you look at the context of James 4, the command to "resist the devil" is associated with something very different. The problem is clear right at the start in James 4:1-2:

> What causes fights and quarrels among you? Don't they come from your desires that battle within you? You desire but do not have, so you kill. You covet but you cannot get what you want, so you quarrel and fight.

James is very clearly warning about wicked desires at work among his audience. But these wicked desires weren't sex, drugs, and rock 'n' roll. No, they were desires that were causing the church to quarrel, fight, and kill. The desires were deemed wicked because they were tempting the church to violence, from the small (quarreling) to the catastrophic (killing). Suddenly, the context of James's admonition to resist the devil becomes very clear: resisting the devil means renouncing conflict and violence, it means "doing battle" with the desires roiling within us—from envy to jealousy to a desire for security—that cause us to fight each other.

The point here is that *the moral is the political*. Consider the virtues associated with the list we know as the "fruits of the spirit" in Galatians 5:22-23: love, joy, peace, forbearance, kindness, goodness, faithfulness, gentleness, and self-control. Look at how social and relational these virtues are. It's pretty hard to be gentle all by yourself. Or kind, or peaceful, or patient, or faithful, or loving. Yes, self-control is in this list, but it comes last, and even self-control affects how we treat each other. Self-control is a critical component in learning how to be patient or loving or gentle. Any difficult interpersonal interaction is going to involve a heap of self-control: mastering your temper, holding your tongue, being patient. Love involves overcoming our innate selfishness, our tendency to think everything is always about us, in order to focus our attention and affections upon others.

All this radically reconfigures what it means to be a *good* or *holy* person. Resisting the devil is what Jesus did when he said "Get behind me, Satan!" It's the same battle we all face when we deny ourselves and take up our own cross to follow Jesus. "Get behind me, Satan!" is living our lives in sacrificial love for others.

Being a holy person is walking as Jesus walked. A *holy* person is a *loving* person.

Consider 1 Peter 1:13-16:

> Therefore, with minds that are alert and fully sober, set your hope on the grace to be brought to you when Jesus Christ is revealed at his coming. As obedient children, do not conform to the evil desires you had when you lived in ignorance. But just as he who called you is holy, so be holy in all you do; for it is written: "Be holy, because I am holy."

We are to resist our evil desires so that we can become holy as God is holy. But what is the goal of holiness? That's revealed a few verses on:

> Now that you have purified yourselves by obeying the truth so that you have sincere love for each other, love one another deeply, from the heart. (1 Peter 1:22)

Notice how the call to holiness—"be holy"—is connected to a very specific goal: purify yourself "so that you have sincere love for each other."

We are called to be holy as God is holy. We are to purify ourselves and pursue holiness so that we might have genuine, sincere, and mutual love for each other. Holiness calls us to become like God.

And if God is love, holiness means increasing our ability and capacity to love. Holiness and purity are the cultivation of love. Again, the holy person is the loving person. The spiritually pure person is the loving person.

The Politics of Sex, Drugs, and Rock & Roll

As a psychologist I have experience working with addictions. So here's another way to illustrate what I'm describing: the chemical is the political. Chemical dependence rips the social and relational fabric that binds our lives together. The same goes for sex. The sexual is the political.

If you've ever seen addiction up close, you've seen how it damages relationships and communities. The life of the addict is filled with lies and broken promises. Everything is sacrificed for the addiction—it leaves behind a trail of failed friendships, marriages, and families. Addiction isn't sinful because God objects to pleasure, it's sinful because it turns us inward upon our selves—what theologians call being *incurvatus in se*, being selfishly "curved inward" upon yourself. Love, by contrast, is being *curved outward* toward others—being available to others, an availability that is impossible in the grip of chemical dependency.

Or when we're in the grip of lust, and consent doesn't protect us from this. I might consent to have sex with you, but I might also want this to be more lasting and deeper than a one-night encounter. I might, heaven forbid, be falling in love with you. And I might want you to fall in love with me. Consent doesn't protect me from the pain and disillusionment when I find I've been used, lied to, rejected, discarded, or betrayed. And consent doesn't protect me from rejection. I might consent to sex but, in that moment when I'm most emotionally and physically exposed and vulnerable, find myself, in subtle or not so subtle ways, shamed or rejected.

The Bible has always linked sex to covenant rather than consent because the writers of the Bible understood that sex is political, relational, and social. Consent is contractual, two isolated individuals negotiating and then reaching an agreement about a sexual transaction. Consent is the child of capitalism. Covenant, by contrast, is *a promise to care for and protect*, tonight, and more importantly, *tomorrow*. The problem with consent is that while we might voluntarily agree to a sexual transaction, and this does protect us from rape and abuse, we might be radically unprepared for how the experience will leave each of us exposed, vulnerable, and needy in ways we hadn't anticipated. Covenant is the promise to care about these exposures, vulnerabilities, and needs.

The issue isn't about pleasure, about the high or orgasm being intrinsically bad. The issue is about love, about how our pursuit of pleasure causes us to hurt each other. When pleasure becomes the goal, people get used and discarded. Just pause to think about all the damage sex has caused in the world or in your own life, from abuse to rape to infidelity to broken promises to sex trafficking to the "adult entertainment" industry. For Christians to shy away from a conversation about sex, fearing we might be lumped in with judgmental Christians, is to turn our backs on the ruinous toll sex takes on our lives. Sexual holiness isn't about puritanism. Sexual holiness is learning how to love and care for each other.

Holy Armor

The Catholic tradition talks a lot about love being chaste. Pure love is a chaste love. And by chaste we mean free from self-interest, a love that is wholly available to others.

Holiness is about making our love chaste so that we might become increasingly available to each other. Holiness, we might say, is the discipline needed to protect our love in a world that is satanically antagonistic to love.

I'm reminded here of how Jesus, in the long prayer he prayed before his arrest and crucifixion, connected holiness with both *mission* and *protection* from the Evil One.

My prayer is not that you take them out of the world but that you protect them from the evil one. They are not of the world, even as I am not of it. Sanctify them by the truth; your word is truth. As you sent me into the world, I have sent them into the world. For them I sanctify myself, that they too may be truly sanctified. (John 17:15-19)

Jesus prays that his followers be made *holy*—sanctified—so that they might be *protected* from the evil one as they are being *sent out* into the world.

As Jesus sees it, holiness provides us with a suit of armor that we need out in the world. Holiness equips us to be missional people. Once again this flips our typical associations with holiness. We tend to think of holiness as being removed from and set apart from the world. But in Jesus' view, *holiness is what allows us to become radically available to the world.* Holiness moves us deeper and deeper *into* the world.

Singing Hope

Yes, we feel tempted by sex or drugs or booze. But we also feel psychologically and spiritually attacked in the face of loss, pain, failure, rejection, and suffering.

The temptations in these instances are less moral—a temptation to sin—than they are an assault upon faith itself, the temptation to give up trusting or believing in the presence or goodness of God. This is the temptation Job faced after Satan attacked him. Sitting in the ashes, Job was tempted to "curse God and die" in the face of all he had lost and was suffering. These are the temptations to anger or despair in the face of suffering and injustice. Spiritual warfare in these moments is less about *holiness* than it is about holding on to our spiritual *foundation*—faith, hope, and love.

I see this side of spiritual warfare a lot out at the prison. Beyond things like addictions and walking the long road to recovery we struggle to hold on to hope. Hope is life-giving, but it can be very, very hard to come by.

Recently a young man, Tomás, joined our prison Bible study. His sentence is life without parole. He's eighteen. Hope is going to be a battle for Tomás. So I want to walk alongside him each week to help him fight that spiritual battle. There will be good days for Tomás and some very dark days. But every day Tomás must resist the devil if he is going to hold on to hope.

And so do I. There are days when hope is very hard for me.

In the years I've spent with the Men in White, we've discovered a potent weapon in our shared battle to hold on to hope. If I were an exorcist this would be my crucifix and holy water.

Singing.

A couple of years ago I noticed on the shelves of the bookcase in the prison chapel a row of old church hymnals. Most of the men in the study have little experience with church, so they weren't using the songbooks. But I grew up in a church that worshiped out of hymnals with congregational singing: "Amazing Grace," "I'll Fly Away," "Leaning on the Everlasting Arms." I knew all these songs. So in the middle of the study I started getting out the songbooks to lead the men in an old-fashioned hymn sing.

Some nights singing is the main thing we do. The men calling out songs and all of us joining in. Singing, I've come to see, is spiritual warfare. Singing is how we come alongside each other to lift our spirits in the midst of darkness and despair. Singing is exorcism. I feel this acutely as our voices ring out in the prison. Some nights I can tell the men are down, depressed, discouraged, despairing. Satan is winning the battle against hope. The men live in a brutal, inhumane place, and some weeks are harder than others. So when I discern the spirits and get a sense that it's been a particularly difficult week, I make sure we pass out the songbooks.

And more weeks than not, I'm the one who needs the singing. When I'm having a hard week I can't wait to get out to the prison to sing with the Men in White. Strange, how I've found a spiritual oasis behind barbed wire.

On those dark nights when we start singing, something changes. The mood becomes more hopeful. Spirits start to lift. Smiles appear. And once we start, we don't want to stop. We keep calling out numbers to hymns and I keep my prepared study notes tucked away. We sing on and on, into the night. It reminds me of Paul and Silas who sang in jail after being beaten and arrested in Philippi:

> The crowd joined in the attack against Paul and Silas, and the magistrates ordered them to be stripped and beaten with rods. After they had been severely flogged, they were thrown into prison, and the jailer was commanded to guard them carefully. When he received these orders, he put them in the inner cell and fastened their feet in the stocks. About midnight Paul and Silas were praying and singing hymns to God, and the other prisoners were listening to them. (Acts 16:22-25)

Savagely beaten, suffering from blood loss and sitting in absolute darkness, Paul and Silas must have been feeling very afraid and close to death.

And so they sang.

They did it because singing is an act of spiritual warfare, resisting the Devil. Just like Paul and Silas, we sing to hold on to hope. We sing in the prison for the same reason the civil rights activists sang in the '50s and '60s as they faced fire hoses and police dogs. And I believe they sang for the same reason that we gather in our churches to sing. We sing to give ourselves courage. We sing to receive anew the grace that found and saved us. We sing so that fear can give way to faith, hope, and love. We sing because singing is the exorcism of fear and despair.

And it's the same out at Freedom. Why does a worship-filled, charismatic spirituality thrive on the margins of society? Why do we dance in Holy Ghost conga lines? The answer should be obvious. When life is hard, we must constantly exorcise the demons of despair. And worship, praise, and testimony are how we combat the despair and reach toward hope.

When I first encountered the Holy Ghost conga lines at Freedom, I was uneasy. I didn't know what to do with such an exuberant and spontaneous display of joy in worship. But now I see more clearly. Just as holiness is a form of moral armor, the worship at Freedom is the armor of hope. We sing out at the prison because singing is our shield.

Holiness and hope.

Theses are shields we take up and the armor we strap on to extinguish the flaming arrows of the Evil One.

Chapter 13

The Lucifer Effect

I TEACH AN adult Bible class at my church on Sunday mornings. A few years ago we were studying the book of 1 Corinthians and we had reached the famous "Love Chapter," 1 Corinthians 13. "Love is patient, love is kind . . ."

It's a great chapter, the Love Chapter, one of the best in the Bible. But it's a tough one to teach because we've heard it so many times that it's hard to make the words and message new and fresh. For over two millennia and across countless wedding homilies, books, and classes, billions of words have been devoted to 1 Corinthians 13. What was I going to say on this particular Sunday morning that could add to the subject?

What more can be said about love?

I pondered that question, and then I made a decision.

I'd start the class by talking about assholes.

Assholes were on my mind because the week I was preparing for my class on 1 Corinthians 13 I had finished a great book by Bob Sutton titled *The No Asshole Rule: Building a Civilized Workplace and*

Surviving One That Isn't.[1] Sutton is a Stanford business professor and in 2004 he was asked to propose a "Breakthrough Idea" for *The Harvard Business Review*'s annual edition devoted to sharing hot, new business insights. As Sutton reflected on his experiences working with businesses and other organizations, he decided to share what he called the "no asshole rule," an inside joke Sutton and some former colleagues used when they contemplated hiring decisions. The workplace Sutton and his colleagues shared was warm and friendly. People liked coming to work and being together. And because of this, the workplace was thriving and productive, people were happy, and the work was getting done.

So when Sutton and his colleagues contemplated a new hire they were concerned about if the new person would mess with the good thing they had going. Was this person going to be mean and nasty? Competitive, selfish, and petty?

So during the interview process, they wanted to weed out jerks, and they dubbed this hiring criterion the No Asshole Rule.

Sutton went on to look around the business world, and he noted that other workplaces practiced their own versions of the No Asshole Rule. These were companies that practiced a Zero Tolerance policy toward rude and nasty behavior in the workplace, that prized and cultivated respectful and kind behavior throughout the company, especially in the interactions between superiors and subordinates. And confirming his own personal experience, Sutton noted that companies that had implemented a version of the No Asshole Rule also thrived in the marketplace. Staying clear of assholes, it seems, is good for business.

So Sutton shared the No Asshole Rule with the *Harvard Business Review*, arguing that companies should address the behavior of mean, nasty, selfish, egomaniacal, and rude persons in the workplace. After publishing his idea in the *Review*, he was overwhelmed

---

1. Robert I. Sutton, *The No Asshole Rule: Building a Civilized Workplace and Surviving One That Isn't* (New York: Warner Business, 2007).

with feedback from people around the globe telling him stories of the toll assholes exact in the workplace. And he also confirmed that companies who had implemented a version of the No Asshole Rule had experienced not only a boost in their corporate culture but to their bottom line as well. All this inspired Sutton to write his book.

What most struck me about *The No Asshole Rule* is how Sutton focuses most of his attention in the book to how superiors treat subordinates in the workplace. How the boss, for example, treats the secretary. Or how a manager treats the janitorial staff. According to Sutton, nastiness in the workplace is mainly associated with issues of hierarchy and power and how hierarchy and power can poison basic human kindness and respect.

For example, how can you identify an asshole in your life or workplace? Sutton proposes two tests:

Test One:
After talking to the alleged asshole, does the "target" feel oppressed, humiliated, de-energized, or belittled by the person? In particular, does the target feel worse about him or herself?

Test Two:
Does the alleged asshole aim his or her venom at people who are less powerful rather than at those people who are more powerful?[2]

If Test One describes what it feels like to interact with an asshole, Test Two describes how assholes tend to operate. Assholes like to wield power over others, belittling, oppressing, bossing around, and generally being nasty to subordinates. A part of implementing the No Asshole Rule levels out or reverses this dynamic, where those higher up the corporate ladder work to treat subordinates with dignity and respect. And as we all know, this is less about *policy* than it is about *people*. Kindness can't be legislated through a memo or a meeting. Kindness is a matter of character. As Sutton powerfully

---

2. Ibid., 9.

summarizes: "The difference between how a person treats the powerless versus the powerful is as good a measure of human character as I know."[3] Amen to that.

Satan Is the #1 Asshole

In Romans 12:2 we read this exhortation: "Do not conform to the pattern of this world." Throughout the Bible spiritual warfare is an act of nonconformity. But that begs the question, what exactly is the "pattern of this world" that I should be resisting?

It's an important question because throughout the Bible Satan is described as being "the ruler" of the world. We've already talked about how Satan takes Jesus up to a mountain and shows him all the kingdoms of the world and their splendor. "I will give you all their authority and splendor," Satan says to Jesus, "for it has been given to me, and I can give it to anyone I want to." In John 12:31 Satan is described as "the prince of this world." 2 Corinthians 4:4 describes Satan as "the god of this world." Finally, in Ephesians 2:2 the "ways of this world" are identified with Satan who is "the ruler of the kingdom of the air."

Our theology of spiritual warfare must give an account of *the world* and how it is regularly described as the domain and kingdom of Satan. Spiritual warfare means stepping out of the world and into the kingdom of God. It means living in the world but not conforming to "the pattern of the world."

On the mountain at the outset of his ministry, Jesus resisted being poured into a satanic mold. Our nonconformity should imitate the new pattern Jesus enacted in the world. Rejecting the "pattern of this world," Jesus marched to the tune of a different drummer—he chose the cadence of the kingdom of God, and to follow him we must trace out the same beat.

When doubting and disenchanted Christians stop talking about the Devil, it becomes harder for them to follow Jesus. Lose track of

---

3. Ibid., 25.

the Devil and you lose track of Jesus. The reason for this should be obvious. If following Jesus is fundamentally an act of *nonconformity* to the world, you need to have a clear sense about what *conformity* to the world looks like. If the kingdom of God is an act of rebellion, you need to know what you're rebelling against. Otherwise you're just walking in circles. This is what it means when Jesus described the Devil as the Prince of the World (John 12:21; 14:40). When we invoke the Devil we are tracing out the pattern of this world so that we can resist conformity to that pattern.

Over and over in the Gospels, Jesus describes and illustrates the pattern of the kingdom of God and how it differs from the pattern of this world. A great example can be found in Matthew 20, when the mother of James and John approaches Jesus with a request: Would Jesus, when he takes ownership of his kingdom, give her two sons powerful and influential positions? Jesus demurs. The pattern of his kingdom is something radically different than what she, or anyone else, imagines. Powerful positions in the kingdom of God? That's like trying to fit a round peg into a square hole. The shape of the kingdom is wholly different from the pattern of the world.

The other disciples hear about the Machiavellian maneuver to get James and John power and influence over them in the kingdom. They're understandably upset that the Sons of Thunder have been positioning themselves behind the scenes for a power grab, and an argument breaks out. Hearing the argument, Jesus steps in, and the gist of what Jesus says is this: This entire argument is based upon a huge misunderstanding. First, you can't make a power grab in the kingdom of God. And second, because you can't make a power grab in the kingdom of heaven it's pointless to get upset about others trying to make a power grab. Power grabs are the "pattern of the world." But the pattern of the kingdom of God is totally different. As Jesus describes it:

> Jesus called them together and said, "You know that the rulers of the Gentiles lord it over them, and their high officials exercise authority over them. Not so with you. Instead, whoever wants to become great among you must be your servant, and whoever

wants to be first must be your slave—just as the Son of Man did not come to be served, but to serve, and to give his life as a ransom for many." (Matthew 20:25-28)

In the world there are assholes. There is power and hierarchy and lording over others. Domination over others, *that* is the pattern of the world. And that's precisely what Jesus turned his back on when he turned down Satan's offer on the mountain. It shall not be that way in the kingdom, Jesus says to the disciples. In the kingdom of God we'll be playing by a different set of rules.

Jesus makes this point over and over and over again in the Gospels. Overhearing a pissing contest between his disciples about who will be the Alpha Male of the kingdom, Jesus huddles up the disciples to share the secret of the kingdom: "Anyone who wants to be first must be the very last, and the servant of all" (Mark 9:33-35). And on the night before he was killed Jesus made this his final, parting message: "You call me 'Teacher' and 'Lord,' and rightly so, for that is what I am. Now that I, your Lord and Teacher, have washed your feet, you also should wash one another's feet" (John 13:13-14).

The pattern of the kingdom of God is not a lording over, where "the greatest" exercise authority over others. The pattern of the kingdom of God is where the King and the Lord is found in the last place, serving others and washing feet.

Spiritual warfare must focus on how unjust power structures—the principalities and powers—harm and oppress others, especially the most vulnerable among us. So we resist the powers and principalities when they act as playground bullies, lording over others. But as we see in the Gospel stories, we're not immune to the allure of power. We're all tempted to be assholes. Craving to be the boss. Desiring to climb the ladder. Jealous to call the shots. Pushing to stand in the position of influence.

On social media we crave more followers, more clicks and bigger platforms. Bigger speaking gigs, a book deal, a church with a bigger congregation, a better title on the business card, a more prestigious college for our kids to attend.

We're all tempted to climb. Because, come on, admit it, don't you think the world would be a better place if you were in charge and everyone did as you told them to?

And isn't that *exactly* the temptation Satan offered Jesus?

Our battle with the principalities and powers isn't just a battle waged out in the world, at locations of political and economic bullying. It's also a deeply personal and spiritual battle, a battle in our own hearts and minds to resist the allure of lording over in our own personal spheres of influence.

Power Breeds Satans

As Bob Sutton points out, assholes are created because we are all so easily corrupted by hierarchy and asymmetries in power. Even the smallest power differentials can transform us into assholes. Sutton describes research by Deborah Gruenfeld, who has extensively studied the ruinous toll of hierarchy on human character. In one study, Gruenfeld observed groups of three individuals asked to discuss a controversial topic. One of the three participants was randomly appointed to evaluate the recommendations of the other two, which meant being placed, as the judge, in a slightly higher power role. Later in the experiment the three participants were brought a plate of five cookies, intentionally an odd number so that only two of the three could help themselves to a second cookie. Here's what the researchers found: Power corrupts. The "high status" participant, the one randomly selected to be the judge, was more likely to take a second cookie, chew with his or her mouth open, and get crumbs on the table. Sutton observes: "This silly study scares me because it shows how having just a slight power edge causes regular people to grab the cookies for themselves and act like rude pigs. Just think about the effects in thousands of interactions every year."[4] In other words, assholes aren't born, they're made. "Power breeds nastiness," Sutton writes.

---

4. Ibid., 72.

Sutton's conclusion—that "power breeds nastiness"—is well known to psychologists. In thinking about how power relations can distort human relations, our minds quickly go to one of the most famous studies in social psychology, the Stanford Prison Study (recently dramatized in a critically acclaimed movie). Conducted in 1971 by Philip Zimbardo, the Stanford Prison Study was famously called off because the guards of a simulated prison, previously well-adjusted young college students, became abusive and sadistic when given power over prisoners. Power bred nastiness. In his book about the Stanford Prison Study, Zimbardo dubbed this dynamic "the Lucifer effect."[5]

The Lucifer effect. That's the diabolical pattern of this world.

Spiritual warfare isn't just about political resistance to oppressive and unjust power structures. It's also about our own thirst for power, status, and influence. We're all tempted and corrupted by "the Lucifer effect," tempted to take a second cookie for ourselves, tempted to make a power grab. Because, deep down, we all think the world would be better off if we were calling the shots.

Spiritual warfare, then, is stepping out of the pattern of the world to conform ourselves to the pattern at work in the kingdom of God. A pattern of life where the last shall be first and where the least of these is exalted as the greatest. A paradoxical kingdom, as the world sees it, where the King rules by being a servant who washes feet.

Kenarchy Rules!

I like the term *kenarchy*, coined by Roger Mitchell, to describe how in the kingdom of God we divest ourselves of power and dominion over others.[6] Combining the Greek words *kenosis* ("emptying") from Philippians 2 and *arche* ("rule"), kenarchy is the "rule"

---

5. Philip G. Zimbardo, *The Lucifer Effect: Understanding How Good People Turn Evil* (New York: Random House, 2007).
6. Roger Haydon Mitchell, *The Fall of the Church* (Eugene, OR: Wipf & Stock, 2013).

or "authority" of love. Kenarchy is the "new politics" of love that Jesus introduces with a kingdom made up of servants who renounce power over others.

A closer look at the Kenosis Hymn in Philippians makes the connection between kenosis and power even clearer:[7]

In your relationships with one another, have the same mindset as Christ Jesus:

Who, being in very nature God,
did not consider equality with God something to be used to his own advantage;
rather, he made himself nothing
by taking the very nature of a servant,
being made in human likeness.
And being found in appearance as a man,
he humbled himself
by becoming obedient to death—
even death on a cross! (Philippians 2:5-8)

It's a mistake to think of kenosis solely as an "emptying" that takes you from the top to the bottom, because that's something only the privileged and powerful can do—which is fine, and no doubt Jesus' example calls upon the powerful to do just that. As Jesus taught his disciples, there is no "lording over" in his kingdom. But kenosis also has a broader meaning that applies to everyone.

Specifically, the Greek phrase *isa Theo*, translated as "equal to god" or "equality with god," was an honorific title given to Caesar (Caesar being considered a god). In fact, Caesar Augustus outlawed cities granting this honorific title—being equal to a god—to anyone other than Caesar. Claiming to be *isa Theo* was a political challenge, a claim that you were a rival to Caesar.

As the Kenosis Hymn declares, King Jesus, whom Christians call the "Lord of all" (Acts 10:36), was *isa Theo*. Jesus was Caesar's

---

7. I owe the following insights to Stephen Backhouse.

equal if not superior. And yet, the Hymn continues, Jesus did not consider this status as something to be *harpagmon*—a Greek word that's a bit tricky to translate. Some translations render it "clung to" or "grasped." But a longer and more literal translation is one from the NIV above: "did not consider it something to be used to his own advantage." This definition of *harpagmon* is key in understanding kenosis, as kenosis is framed in the Hymn as the opposite of *harpagmon*. *Harpagmon* literally means to seize something as plunder with an open use of force. *Harpagmon* is a term with military overtones, a term of power and violence.

Harpagmon is the Lucifer effect. *Harpagmon* is taking that extra cookie for yourself. *Harpagmon* is what Bob Sutton was trying to call out in his book the *No Asshole Rule*. *Harpagmon* is the power grab, writ small and large across our lives. From the seemingly inconsequential act of taking that extra cookie for ourselves to our craving to be "the greatest," to lording over others in oppressive and domineering ways.

And beyond the personal temptations we face in our intimate spheres of influence, we also need to pay attention to the temptations we encounter as doubting and disenchanted Christians when we reduce spiritual warfare to political activism. When spiritual warfare is reduced to a political struggle, it becomes the power grab of *harpagmon*. The power grab where the Good Guys take power away from the Bad Guys so that the Good Guys can lord over and rule the world.

This is the exact offer Satan made to Jesus on the mountain. All that power was rightfully Jesus'. As King and Lord of all Jesus was clearly *isa Theo*, the equal if not the superior to Caesar, who was the Big Boss of the World. But in renouncing the Devil, in not conforming to the pattern of the world, Jesus pushed back on the Lucifer effect. Jesus renounced *harpagmon* in favor of kenosis. Jesus did not consider his rightful status as *isa Theo* as something to be seized and taken by force. Jesus rejected the "pattern of this world" and chose, instead, to rule as one who "takes on the form of a servant." What Jesus rejects on the mountain isn't his *status* as *isa Theo*. What Jesus rejects is *harpagmon*, using his power and status to lord over others. Kenosis is not a movement from "high" status to "low" status but a refusal to use coercive power in the world to seize and take things for ourselves. Instead of seizing and gathering power for himself, as Roman political rivals did as they plotted against Caesar seeking to be his *isa Theo* equal, Jesus renounced this path and chose the path of love.

The whole Kenosis Hymn dynamic is there in the Gospel account of Jesus washing the disciples' feet. In the words of John 13, Jesus "knew that the Father had put all things under his power." Jesus knew he was *isa Theo*, and more. Jesus had all the power in the world. But Jesus didn't use that power for his own advantage. Jesus renounced Satan on the mountain. And on the night he was betrayed, Jesus showed us exactly what saying no to Satan looks like:

"He got up from the meal, took off his outer clothing, and wrapped a towel around his waist."

And that was Jesus' command to his followers, "Now that I, your Lord and Teacher, have washed your feet, you also should wash one another's feet."

That towel around Jesus' waist and ours? That's the No Asshole Rule. That's how Satan's temptation on the mountain is finally and decisively renounced.

The towel around our waist is how we resist the Lucifer effect. Washing feet is how we resist conforming to the pattern of this world.

Chapter 14

The One Who Holds the Power of Death

A COUPLE OF years ago my wife and I spent a few days in contemplative retreat at a Benedictine monastery. One afternoon during our stay there we stopped by the small bookstore at the monastery. We made a few purchases and as we were checking out, the sister helping us handed us a few St. Benedict Medals. "Here, have some of these," she said. "They are Medals of St. Benedict." I took them and thanked her. Then she said, "They give protection from evil."

Well, that caught my attention. Who doesn't want to be protected from evil? So when I got back home from the monastery I did a little research about the Medal of St. Benedict. I wanted to know why this particular medal was associated with protection from Old Scratch.

The medal has two sides. On the front of the medal is an image of Benedict himself. In his left hand he's holding a copy of *The Rule of St. Benedict*, the founding document of Christian monasticism, and in his right hand he is holding a cross aloft. Around the edge of the medal are the words *Ejus in obitu nostro presentia muniamur*, "May we be protected by his presence in the hour of death." Due to the peace of his own death, Benedict is considered a patron saint of the dying, and the medal is often used in ministering to the sick and dying.

On the backside of the medal are references to the Devil. The back of the medal is dominated by a cross. On the vertical bar of the cross are the letters C, S, S, M, and L. On the horizontal bar of the cross are the letters N, D, S, M, D. Taken together these letters stand for the Latin words *Crux Sacra Sit Mihi Lux—Non Draco Sit Mihi Dux*: "May the Sacred Cross be my light—Let not the dragon be my guide."

Around the border of the back of the medal are the letters V, R, S, N, S, M, V—S, M, Q, L, I, V, B. These letters stand for the Latin words *Vade Retro Satana! Nunquam Suade Mihi Vana! Sunt Mala Quae Libas. Ipse Venena Bibas!* "Begone Satan! Never tempt me with your vanities! Evil is the cup you offer. Drink the poison yourself!" And it's here with this explicit command to Satan—"Begone Satan!"—that we see why the Medal of St. Benedict is associated with protection from the Devil.

What's interesting about the Medal of St. Benedict is how the front side of the medal is associated with being protected from *our fear of death* and the backside is associated with protection from *the power of the Devil*. That connection is no accident, and it illustrates how the early church thought about God's rescue operation in Christus Victor, the view of Jesus' death that we explored earlier. Specifically, the power of the Devil in our lives isn't some sort of diabolical craving, like the allure of sex or some other carnal pleasure. Instead, according to the early church the power of the Devil was *death* and how Satan uses our fear of death to make us selfish and violent. The Devil uses our fear of death to keep tempting and bullying us into sin.

Setting us free from the power of the Devil is setting us free from our fear of death and how that fear interferes with our ability to love each other, fully, spontaneously, and sacrificially. The whole Christus Victor dynamic is succinctly described in the book of Hebrews:

> Since the children have flesh and blood, [Christ Jesus] too shared in their humanity so that by his death he might break the power of him who holds the power of death—that is, the devil—and free those who all their lives were held in slavery by their fear of death. (Hebrews 2:14-15)

Jesus comes to break the power of the Devil, the one who holds the power of death, to set us free from our slavery to the fear of death. In order to rescue us from bondage, Jesus has to set us free from both Satan and death. That's exactly what Aslan does in *The Lion, the Witch and the Wardrobe*, he defeats the White Witch by cracking the Stone Table, the power of death. Aslan dies and comes back to life so that the "Table would crack and Death itself would start working backwards."

Open the Doors!

In the early church, the defeat of death was called the "harrowing of Hell," an obscure little doctrine built on a handful of texts (1 Peter 3:18-20; 4:6; Eph. 4:8-10) that suggest that after his death, Jesus descended into hell to set free all the people, beginning with Adam and Eve, who had died and who were being held captive in hell by the Devil. Christus Victor atonement was a grand rescue operation to set free hostages and captives. Jesus descends into hell to break everyone out of the Devil's jail. Jesus busts the Devil and takes the Keys of Death away from him. Jesus, in the words of Revelation, now holds the "keys to death and hades." Death, the power of the Devil, has been defeated. The Stone Table has been cracked.

You might find the Harrowing of Hell, as a doctrine, either weird or delightful. I have a Harrowing of Hell icon in my office, and it always makes me smile. I like the image of Jesus going down into hell to rumble with the Devil. But I'm not merely entertained by the Harrowing of Hell, there's also an important theological insight at the heart of the doctrine.

The Harrowing of Hell is so important to the Eastern Orthodox Church that they reenact it during their Easter liturgy. The priest exits the church with a cross held high, and the congregation remains inside. The church doors are locked and the lights are turned off. The darkened church becomes hell, the Devil's jail. The priest then pounds on the doors of the church—symbolizing Christ assaulting the gates of Hades—proclaiming "Open the doors to the Lord of the powers, the king of glory!" Inside the church the people make a great noise of rattling chains, the resistance of hell to the coming of Christ. Eventually the doors are opened, the cross enters, and the church is lit and filled with incense. For the Orthodox, Easter is all about how Jesus defeats the power of death. And the Harrowing of Hell is a critical part of this.

For doubting and disenchanted Christians it might be hard to see the practical implications of the Harrowing of Hell. The vision of Christ raiding Hades is fascinating but hard for doubting Christians to get their head around. But remember that text from Hebrews: the power the Devil—death—is *emotional* in nature. In the words of Hebrews, Christ sets us free from our slavery to the *fear* of death. Emancipation from our fear of death is critical because, as we read in 1 John 4:18, perfect love must cast out fear. Love is experiencing a resurrected life, a life set free from the fear of death, set free from the power of the Devil.

I keep a Harrowing of Hell icon in my office to remind me of the power of the Devil at work in my life. My slavery to the fear of death must be cast out—exorcised—if perfect love is to reign in my life, a love that moves me from death to life. Spiritual warfare is battling against the power of the Devil. Which means that spiritual warfare is becoming emancipated from our slavery to the fear of death so that we can experience love and resurrection.

The Fear of Death

But here's the problem. I wrote a book about all this titled *The Slavery of Death*.[1] And as I've gone around talking about the book I've encountered two sorts of reactions. The first reaction is from people who have an acute sense of death anxiety. These people totally get the message about our slavery to the fear of death. For example, many years ago a friend of mine emailed me after the birth of his first child. He asked me, "Is it normal, as a new parent, to have your death anxiety increase after the birth of your child?" I told my friend that I knew of no research on the topic but that was precisely my experience when Brenden, my oldest son, was born. Looking at my tiny baby boy, so small and vulnerable, I realized how joyful my life had become but also how fragile. All my happiness was being poured into that baby and he seemed like such a vulnerable container. Vulnerable to illness and accident. And I knew that if anything happened to Brenden my life would be forever changed, traumatically scarred with pain and loss. When Brenden was born I was never happier. But I was scared as well. And I've never stopped being scared. It used to be high fevers that would make me anxious. Now that Brenden is a teenager it's not being able to rest well until I know his car has pulled into the driveway and he's safely back at home. Being a parent is joyful, but it's also haunted by the specter of loss.

I've found the research of Brené Brown helpful in understanding this connection between joy and fear. In Brown's research she has asked people about when they have felt the most vulnerable and exposed to loss. And more often than not what people have shared with her are experiences of great joy. According to Brown, these are the sorts of experiences in life that make us feel most vulnerable:

- Standing over my children while they are sleeping.
- Acknowledging how much I love my husband/wife.

---

1. Richard Beck, *The Slavery of Death* (Eugene, OR: Cascade, 2013).

- Knowing how good I've got it.
- Loving my job.
- Spending time with my parents.
- Getting engaged.
- Going into remission.
- Having a baby.
- Being happy.
- Falling in love.[2]

Joy and a fear of loss go hand in hand.

Brown goes on to describe how many of us cope with these fears and anxieties. We practice what Brown calls "foreboding joy." According to Brown, we practice foreboding joy by emotionally withdrawing from joy so that we might protect ourselves from disappointment. Brown describes a continuum of strategies here, from "rehearsing tragedy" to "perpetual disappointment," from ruminating about worst-case scenarios to keeping our expectations very, very low. According to Brown, all these strategies share a central idea: "We're trying to beat vulnerability to the punch. We don't want to be blindsided by hurt. We don't want to be caught off-guard, so we literally practice being devastated or never move from self-elected disappointment."[3]

As I've gone around talking about our slavery to the fear of death, many people in the audience immediately get what I'm talking about. These are the people practicing foreboding joy, people who are acutely aware that life and happiness are fragile and vulnerable, that it all can be swept away in an instant. And in order to protect ourselves from that pain we start emotionally withdrawing from life. We put armor around our hearts so we won't get hurt. The fear of loss, failure, and disappointment haunts our every step. Fear starts

---

2. Brené Brown, *Daring Greatly: How the Courage to Be Vulnerable Transforms the Way We Live, Love, Parent, and Lead* (New York: Gotham, 2012), 119.

3. Ibid., 121.

to erode our ability to love, because love is inherently risky. Love leaves us exposed and vulnerable. And in our fear we pull back. We begin to live enslaved to the fear of the death.

The Feeling of Lack

The other reaction that I get when I talk about our slavery to the fear of death is confusion and incomprehension. Lots of people, it seems, don't think about death at all, so bringing up death or the potential for loss seems unnecessarily morbid and depressing. It's not that they don't admit the possibility of death, just that they don't feel particularly *enslaved* to the fear of death. And it's hard to be convinced that you're enslaved to something you don't think or worry much about.

So this is what I say to those in my audience who don't think they live enslaved to the fear of death. "You might not think a lot about death," I say. "But how many of you are tired and exhausted? Raise your hands."

As you might guess, just about every hand in the room goes up.

Pastors and preachers talk a lot about living a radical life for Jesus. We don't want to be a fan of Jesus, but a radical, all-in, fired-up, 110 percent committed follower of Jesus. But do you know what most of the people sitting in the pews hear when they hear the word "radical" from the pulpit and stage? This:

You're making me tired.

People walk into Sunday-morning assemblies feeling tired and depleted. We're running on fumes. Our tanks are empty. So when we hear words like "radical" we just don't know how we're going to find the time or energy to fit that into our busy, exhausted, over-scheduled lives.

It might not seem like exhaustion is a manifestation of our fear of death, but it is. Our worries about exhaustion are all about being physically and biologically worn down and depleted. And when physical resources are running low we grow worried and anxious. You have to if you want to survive.

Basically, we encounter our fear of death whenever we run up against our limitations. Brené Brown calls this the "never enough" problem, a worry rooted in our concerns about scarcity. In her book *Daring Greatly* here's how Brown describes our experience of scarcity:

> Scarcity is the "never enough" problem. . . . Scarcity thrives in a culture where everyone is hyperaware of lack. Everything from safety and love to money and resources feels restricted or lacking. We spend inordinate amounts of time calculating how much we have, want, and don't have, and how much everyone else has, needs, and wants.[4]

That assessment, scarcity is a culture where everyone is "hyperaware of lack," is personally and politically potent. Politically because we know that America is a culture driven by fear. And when you explore the roots of that fear you find that they are rooted in concerns about scarcity. Fears that undermine our collective ability to create a fair and hospitable social contract. Fearing that jobs and opportunities are scarce we fret about immigration, fearing that the immigrant will take a job or opportunity away from us. Fearing that money is scarce we fret about wasteful government spending, especially spending upon those we consider to be undeserving. And fearing that safety is scarce we demand that walls be built along our borders and that our military police the entire world for threats. Just turn on cable TV and you'll see the whole dynamic play out on a nightly basis. Fears rooted in a culture of scarcity undermine our ability to love each other.

We also experience scarcity on a more personal level. We're constantly struggling with the never-enough problem. I like how Lynn Twist describes how most of us feel on a daily basis:

> For me, and for many of us, our first waking thought of the day is "I didn't get enough sleep." The next one is "I don't have enough time." Whether true or not, that thought of not enough

---

4. Ibid., 25, 26.

occurs to us automatically before we even think to question or examine it. We spend most of the hours and the days of our lives hearing, explaining, complaining, or worrying about what we don't have enough of.... Before we even sit up in bed, before our feet touch the floor, we're already inadequate, already behind, already losing, already lacking something. And by the time we go to bed at night, our minds are racing with a litany of what we didn't get, or didn't get done, that day. We go to sleep burdened by those thoughts and wake up to that reverie of lack.... This internal condition of scarcity, this mind-set of scarcity, lives at the very heart of our jealousies, our greed, our prejudice, and our arguments with life.[5]

We all can relate to this reverie of lack. There's the physical experience of lack: not enough sleep, time, or energy. Not enough money to pay the bills. But there's also a lack that relates to our self-esteem: not enough success, influence, or recognition affects our feelings of worthiness and usefulness. We experience the never-enough problem in two different ways: not *having* enough and not *being* enough. And both sorts of scarcity create fears that undermine our ability to love. Scarcity becomes the power of the Devil in our lives.

These two experiences of scarcity—not *having* enough and not *being* enough—affect our ability to love each other, fully, joyfully, and sacrificially.

Let's start with the experience of not being enough, our feelings of inadequacy and insecurity on the one hand and our thirst for recognition and praise on the other, what Brené Brown calls "the shame-based fear of being ordinary."

As Henri Nouwen once wrote, the world presents us with three great temptations, the temptation to be relevant, the temptation to be spectacular, and the temptation to be powerful.[6] Nobody wants to

---

5. Ibid., 25.
6. Henri Nouwen, *The Selfless Way of Christ* (Maryknoll, NY: Orbis, 2007), 48–49.

be ordinary. Or average. Nobody wants to be the last one picked for the kickball game. Nobody wants to be the failure or the loser. And so we push to stand out from the crowd. We crave success, applause, and attention. We want to have influence, a platform, a voice.

Because we struggle with not being enough, we're always being tempted to act like the disciples in the Gospels as they repeatedly argue with each other about who would be the greatest in the kingdom. We might not publicly air our jealousies or ambitions like the disciples did—we're much too sophisticated for that—but we're often struggling inside ourselves with the very same issues. And even if we're not struggling for attention and influence, we're crippled by shame or feelings of inadequacy. Fears of not being enough—not being successful enough or worthy enough—flood our lives.

And these fears compromise our ability to love each other. After Jesus caught the disciples arguing about who among them would be the greatest in the kingdom, he told them that the greatest among them would be the servant, that the first would be the last. But that move is very hard to make if we're crippled by a shame-based fear of being ordinary. Thirsting as we do to take center stage and stand in the limelight, it's hard to step out of the spotlight and serve in small and unnoticed ways. Our desire to be powerful, spectacular, and relevant undercuts our ability to follow Jesus into a lifestyle of washing feet.

It's the same problem we struggle with when it comes to marginalizing our privilege, power, or position as we focus on the voices and concerns of those who have been marginalized and oppressed. Even our social justice efforts become contaminated by our desire to be the center of attention as we fail to place weaker and less powerful voices at the center of our concerns.

We also experience scarcity in feeling like we just don't *have* enough. In 1 John where we're told that perfect love casts out fear, we're also told that love involves laying down our lives for each other, which is a scary prospect. When you're already feeling depleted and exhausted, the call to "lay down our lives for each other" feels like a kick in the gut. We're running on fumes. We just don't have anything left to give. We just don't have it in us.

When we're running on fumes our scarcity is less about our ego and feelings of inadequacy than it is about being physically, materially, and emotionally *unable to carry the burden of love.* Love asks us to share—our time, energy, and stuff—and when we feel like we don't have enough—enough time, energy, or money to pay our own bills let alone anyone else's—we struggle to share freely, joyfully, and sacrificially.

And this only gets worse when your compassion and concern for social justice moves you to the margins of society. The social and material needs you encounter on the margins of society are vast and unending. Your compassion draws you into this need, but you quickly become overwhelmed. I don't have enough money to pay everyone's rent or electric bill. And there are people in my life who need social support and friendship but who, because of addiction, mental illness, or trauma, require extraordinary amounts of time and energy. Loving one person well can totally exhaust you. Especially if you're fighting a heroic battle just to keep your own shit together.

Schindler's Lament

I call this dilemma Schindler's Lament, taking the illustration from the final scene of the movie *Schindler's List*. Oskar Schindler saved over 1,100 Jews from the Holocaust by keeping them employed in his factory. To save workers during the war, Schindler often had to sell his own property and possessions. At the conclusion of the movie the war has ended and Schindler faces all the workers in his factory whom he has saved. But instead of feeling exultant Schindler grows distressed, questioning and lamenting why he didn't do more to save one more person, why didn't he sell more of his stuff to save more workers:

> "I could have gotten more out. I could have got more. . . . If
> I had made more money. I threw away so much money. . . . I

didn't do enough. . . . This car. Why did I keep this car? Ten people right there. Ten people. Ten more people. This pin. Two people. This is gold. Two more people. They would at least have given me one. One more person . . . I could have got one more person. And I didn't. I didn't."[7]

I think any compassionate person in a world of hunger and homelessness can identify with Schindler's lament. We could always do more to save one more person. And one more after that. Compassion seems to pull us toward never-ending sacrifice. We perform the calculus of love in our hearts and the cost just seems to skyrocket, with no end in sight. And as the cost rises so does our anxiety. We fear that if we pay the price of love nothing will be left over. Love crashes into our fears about scarcity.

One possible rebuttal is how this model of benevolence privileges the isolated individual as an agent of charity. Of course one person can't save the entire world. We need to talk about social structures, systems, and sustainability. I agree that Christianity is best expressed in locally rooted and ecologically sustainable communities of mutual care and aid. But let's not kid ourselves. These communities have their own high costs, demands that scare us and cause us to pull away. And in the meantime we'll still get asked this week to help with an unpaid bill or be drawn into a friendship that is going to demand an extraordinary amount of time and energy. And most of the time, if I'm honest, I just don't feel like I have it in me to help any more people.

This fear of scarcity is what it looks like to be enslaved to the fear of death, a fear that is the power of the Devil as it undermines, at every turn, our ability and willingness to love each other. Thirsting for attention, we don't want to wash feet. Crippled by shame, we pull away from others. Running on empty, we pull back from the needs of the world fearing that we'll be exhausted and used up.

---

7. *Schindler's List*, directed by Steven Spielberg. Universal, 2004.

We're hobbled and incapacitated by fear. Which is why perfect love must cast out and exorcize fear. In order to love we must be set free from the power of the Devil.

Exorcizing My Fear

As a doubting and disenchanted Christian, I've always struggled with worship and prayer. Prayer never made much sense to me. It's always seemed like a magic trick, like rubbing the genie's lamp to grant me three wishes. Plus, if God already knows what I need, why do I need to pray?

My attitude toward worship was no better. Is God so insecure that we need to tell him, over and over, just how awesome and amazing he is? And I couldn't figure out how experiencing an overwhelming sense of God's awesomeness in worship was going to make me a better person or the world a better place. Worshiping God as AWE-SOME!!!!!!!!! might make me feel *smaller*, but I've never been clear about how that feeling makes me a better *lover* of God and people.

However, thanks to the prison and Freedom my attitudes toward worship and prayer have been changing. The charismatic spirituality I've encountered in those communities has taught me that worship and prayer are practices of gratitude and joy that combat my mindset of scarcity. The practices of worship and prayer place me in a receptive posture where I receive myself and everything in my life as grace and gift, and an experience of abundance displaces my reverie of lack. And as I experience gratitude, gift, grace, and abundance, the fears that have crippled my love are cast out and exorcised. I become set free from the power of death. In worship and prayer I am emancipated from the power of the Devil. I am being liberated by joy.

And while the Spirit-filled worship of Freedom cracked open my heart, charismatic worship is only one of the ways we come to exorcise our fears. Again, the goal is to replace the experience of scarcity with an experience of gift, gratitude, joy, and abundance.

And the key practices in this regard are those that cultivate what David Kelsey has called *doxological gratitude*.[8]

Psychologists will tell you that gratitude is one of the strongest, if not the strongest, predictors of happiness. And why is that? Because to feel grateful is to experience life as a gift, as an experience of grace and joy. Simple practices of thanksgiving—where we receive life as a gift—replace scarcity with an experience of abundance. When life is experienced as a gift our "reverie of lack" dissipates and our fears are exorcised. Gratitude is the experience that, in Christ, I *have* and *am* "enough." When I practice gratitude I begin to operate out of a sense of abundance rather than scarcity, acting out of joy rather than fear.

And you don't need to dance in a Holy Ghost conga line to do this. Gratitude is a simple practice. One of my favorite studies about gratitude is the "Count Your Blessings" study conducted by the psychologist Bob Emmons.[9] I remember singing the old gospel hymn "Count Your Blessings" as a child. The admonition of the song seemed so simplistic and trite:

> When upon life's billows you are tempest-tossed,
> When you are discouraged, thinking all is lost,
> Count your many blessings, name them one by one,
> And it will surprise you what the Lord has done.
>
> Count your blessings, name them one by one,
> Count your blessings, see what God has done!
> Count your blessings, name them one by one,
> Count your many blessings, see what God has done.

Turns out those lyrics are cutting-edge science. In his "Count Your Blessings" study Emmons had participants do the simplest thing: At

---

8. David H. Kelsey, *Eccentric Existence, Vol. 1* (Louisville: Westminster John Knox, 2009).

9. For more about this study and the science of gratitude see Robert A. Emmons, *Thanks!: How the New Science of Gratitude Can Make You Happier* (Boston: Houghton Mifflin, 2007).

the end of each day take a moment to count your blessings by writing them down in a journal. And you know what happened? At the end of the study the participants who engaged in this simple practice of thanksgiving where healthier—emotionally and physically—than the control group. Simply counting your blessings made people healthier and happier. That's the cheapest therapy you're ever going to find.

Prayer, as a practice, is a constant posture of thankfulness. Prayer is the mindful discipline to act out of an experience of gift rather than scarcity. So count your blessings. Name them, one by one.

But there is more to this than simple thankfulness. In the Bible thanksgiving is always rooted in *doxology*, an expression of praise and worship. And the point of worship isn't to dance in the aisles as we do at Freedom. The point of worship is *allegiance*, the confrontation of our idolatry. I'll talk more about idolatry in the next chapter, but recall our discussion in chapter 11 on how we need to "discern the spirits" in order to give our ultimate allegiance to the kingdom of God. Remember Moses' request to Pharaoh: "Let my people go free to *worship*!" Remember also Daniel defiantly praying in Babylon and Shadrach, Meshach, and Abednego refusing to bow to Nebuchadnezzar's idol. *Worship is the practice of spiritual defiance.* The praise of God—whether you are dancing in the aisles or praying a litany from *The Book of Common Prayer*—is spiritual revolt and resistance. Doxology is *the renunciation of the gods of this world* and pledging allegiance to the kingdom of God.

Worship exorcises our fears because it calls out all the idolatrous ways we try to escape "the shame-based fear of being ordinary," our scarcity-based fears that we aren't good enough, smart enough, strong enough, successful enough. The practices of doxology dismantle the fear- and shame-based ways our world—a world we buy into—pursues meaning, significance, value, and self-esteem.

Worship exposes all our efforts at self-*glorification* and self-*justification*, all the accomplishments and talents we like to parade before others to make them think we're someone special. In worship our pursuit of self-esteem, social standing, and significance—the games we play trying to be relevant, spectacular, and powerful in the eyes of the world—is renounced. In worship we are enough, just as we are, before God. From God we *receive*—gift again!—our identities as beloved children, people no longer reliant upon our talents, accomplishments, abilities, and successes. In worship the power of the Devil—our deepest fears and insecurities that we are not enough—are exorcised.

If practiced mindfully and intentionally the simple practices of doxological gratitude create the emotional and spiritual capacities required to respond to each other joyfully, spontaneously, and gratuitously. Because without that joy nothing gets accomplished. Politically and personally, nothing is going to change if we remain locked in a mindset of scarcity and slaves to fear. Without a spiritual foundation of joyful, grateful spontaneity there's no risk, no thirst for adventure; no willingness to experiment with new and creative forms of community and care; no willingness to sacrifice for each other, especially when it hurts. Without joy and gratitude there is only paranoia, fear, and hesitation, just the dark shadow of scarcity and the reverie of lack. Just the power of the Devil.

As we count our blessings and renounce idols in prayer and worship, the demons of "never enough" are cast out and exorcised. Receiving all things as gift and renouncing our shame-based efforts at self-justification, we experience the abundance of God's grace. All is gift. With God there is always enough.

As we kneel contemplatively or raise our hands ecstatically, in prayer and praise, our reverie of lack begins to lift. That is the harrowing of hell, the power of the Devil defeated and exorcised. Perfect love casting out fear. The Stone Table cracked within our hearts.

Chapter 15

Turning the World Upside Down

EXORCISMS ARE ABOUT economics.

That might sound strange, because when we think of exorcisms we think of things like crucifixes, holy water, and spitting pea soup. You've seen *The Exorcist*, right? When we think of exorcism we don't think of stock portfolios, profit margins, and financial spreadsheets.

But when you read through the book of Acts, that collection of stories about the early followers of Jesus, whenever there's an exorcism, a riot breaks out. And the riots are always about someone losing money. Casting out the Devil affects the marketplace.

The first story about one of these riots happens in the city of Philippi. In Acts 16 Luke, the narrator, tells the story about Paul, Silas, and companions running into a spirit-possessed slave girl who "earned a good fortune for her owners by fortune-telling." Because of her supernatural insight the girl knows who Paul is. So the girl follows Paul and his companions around shouting, "These men are servants of the Most High God, who are telling you the way to be saved." For some reason, because of all the shouting or because the girl was one big Spoiler-Alert, Paul gets fed up. He turns on the girl and performs an exorcism: "In the name of Jesus Christ I command you to come out of her!"

So why does a riot break out? Well, here's what happens next:

> When the owners of the slave girl realized that *their hope of making money was gone*, they seized Paul and Silas and dragged them into the marketplace to face the authorities. They brought them before the magistrates and said, "These men are Jews, and are throwing our city into an uproar by advocating customs unlawful for us Romans to accept or practice."
>
> The crowd joined in the attack against Paul and Silas, and the magistrates ordered them to be stripped and beaten. After they had been severely flogged, they were thrown into prison. (Acts 16:20-23, italics added)

Exorcism had an *economic* impact! Demon possession was associated with economic exploitation. Evil spirits at work in the markets. The coming of God's kingdom affecting the bottom line of the Excel spreadsheet.

Notice also something really important in the story. Notice how the real reason for the riot—"their hope of making money was gone"—was *hidden* by an appeal to God-and-country patriotism: "These men are Jews . . . advocating customs unlawful for us Romans to accept or practice."

A second example is about a riot that breaks out in the city of Ephesus. Magic was big business in Ephesus: spells, charms, amulets, statues, totems, and magic scrolls were used for just about everything—from blessing a business venture to healing a disease. But as the kingdom of God began to make inroads into Ephesus, the magic business took a heavy hit.

The story is told in Acts 19. Some Jewish exorcists, seeing the power displayed by Paul, were invoking the name of Jesus in their own exorcisms. One day, however, the seven sons of Sceva, a Jewish

High Priest, were trying to cast out a demon from a man by invoking the name of Paul and Jesus. But the demon responded, "Jesus I know, and Paul I know about, but who are you?" The demon-possessed man then jumped on them and beat them.

Word about this botched exorcism gets around town. And about the power of Jesus over demons. Consequently, many of Ephesians convert to Christianity and in doing so make a huge bonfire to burn all their magic stuff:

> A number who had practiced sorcery brought their scrolls together and burned them publicly. When they calculated the value of the scrolls, the total came to fifty thousand drachmas. (Acts 19:19)

That's 50,000 silver coins worth of magic stuff going up in smoke.

Historians say that a drachma was about a day's wage. It's hard to translate the value of the ancient drachma into U.S. dollars, but let's attempt a rough, albeit nonscientific, estimate. If you divide 50,000 drachmas by 365 days you have the annual incomes of 137 people, conservatively estimated (no vacation, no days off). The median U.S. annual income in the U.S. in 2014 was just shy of $52,000. So, $52,000 times 137 people equals $7,124,000. Yes, that's right. Over $7 million.

That calculation is close enough to make the point: That was a million-dollar bonfire in Ephesus, maybe even a multi-million-dollar bonfire.

And markets will tend to notice millions of dollars going up in flames.

Sure enough, they did. The markets in Ephesus got spooked and anxious. And predictably, that economic anxiety spills over into violence. Another riot breaks out. It starts with a silversmith:

> About that time there arose a great disturbance about the Way.
>
> A silversmith named Demetrius, *who made silver shrines of Artemis, brought in a lot of business for the craftsmen there.* He

called them together, along with the workers in related trades, and said:

"You know, my friends, that *we receive a good income from this business*. And you see and hear how this fellow Paul has convinced and led astray large numbers of people here in Ephesus and in practically the whole province of Asia. He says that gods made by human hands are no gods at all. *There is danger not only that our trade will lose its good name, but also that the temple of the great goddess Artemis will be discredited*; and the goddess herself, who is worshiped throughout the province of Asia and the world, will be robbed of her divine majesty."

When they heard this, they were furious and began shouting: "Great is Artemis of the Ephesians!" Soon the whole city was in an uproar. The people seized Gaius and Aristarchus, Paul's traveling companions from Macedonia, and all of them rushed into the theater together. (Acts 19:23-29, italics added)

Again, it's a fascinating mixture: Paul's power over demons prompting a multi-million-dollar disruption in the magic trade which, in turn, threatens the idol market. The reason for the riot is the exact same one we noted in Philippi, loss of money. But notice again, in a point we'll come back to, how the economic reasons for the riot— "we receive a good income from this business"—were hidden again by another appeal to god-and-country patriotism: "Great is Artemis of the Ephesians!"

It's difficult to disentangle the political and economic aspects of our battle with the principalities and powers from the underlying spiritual struggle. Both conservative and progressive Christians tend to miss how these are two sides of the same coin. Conservatives tend to focus exclusively upon the spiritual aspects of spiritual warfare. This "spiritualizes" the struggle, which drains it of any political or economic impact or import. Spiritual warfare in the hands of many conservative Christians reduces it to something spooky, fretting about disembodied spirits floating around in the air. Progressive Christians, by contrast, tend to ignore the spiritual aspects of the struggle, focusing exclusively upon the political and economic arena. Where conservatives *spiritualize* spiritual warfare, progressives *politicize* the struggle. So when it comes to the riots in Acts, both groups overlook the spirituality of political and economic systems, how these systems are supported and animated by values, morals, worldviews, and cultural norms, that economies are guided by a spirit—a Zeitgeist—an unseen and animating spiritual center. That's the critical piece of the puzzle doubting and disenchanted Christians miss when they stop talking about the Devil and spiritual warfare.

The animating spiritual center—the spiritual heart and soul of civic life in Philippi and Ephesus—is precisely what was being disrupted by the coming of the kingdom of God in the book of Acts. And since doubting and disenchanted Christians miss this, they miss what was and is so subversive and unsettling about the kingdom of God. Consequently, doubting and disenchanted Christians can't locate the key to unlock one of the great paradoxes of the book of Acts—the secret to the kingdom's revolutionary, riot-inducing power.

Turning the World Upside Down

That paradox is the same paradox we observed with Jesus. As we noted, Jesus wasn't much of an activist. Jesus preached "love your enemies" and appeared to have a soft spot for Roman centurions and tax collectors, agents of imperial oppression. And when Jesus did engage in direct action it was clearing out the temple so that it could be restored as a place of worship.

And yet, Jesus was executed by the state, so clearly there was something subversive about Jesus.

We see something similar in the book of Acts.[1] As they went from city to city, the apostles and the early followers of Jesus didn't

---

1. The argument that follows owes a great deal to: C. Kavin Rowe, *World Upside Down: Reading Acts in the Graeco-Roman Age* (Oxford: Oxford University Press, 2009).

lead marches or hold vigils protesting Roman oppression. They seemed, on the whole, to pay little if any attention to Rome. In fact, in the final chapters of the book of Acts Paul is repeatedly brought before Roman tribunals and officials, and each time they struggle to find concrete evidence for any subversive activity. On the face of it the church wasn't a threat to Rome.

And yet, when the kingdom proclamation reached these new cities in the Roman Empire, riots broke out. Something revolutionary and subversive was happening with the Jesus movement. The book of Acts portrays the gospel proclamation as socially, politically, and economically disruptive. In Acts 17, when another riot breaks out in the city of Thessalonica, the people exclaim that the followers of Jesus are "turning the world upside down."

The church *was* turning the world upside down. Throwing city after city into political and economic chaos. Holy hell breaking out.

Despite a lack of overt antagonism, the Roman Empire came to see the Christian church as a threat, targeting Christians for persecution. Paul was beheaded. Christians were thrown to lions. Followers of Jesus were killed in gladiator games.

This is the paradox of Jesus. Rome had trouble officially locating a treasonous element in Jesus and his followers, but riots broke out. The church was turning the world upside down. Something revolutionary was happening, but Rome had trouble seeing what it was. And I think we have the same problem. It's hard for us to nail down exactly *why* the church was so subversive and revolutionary.

What happened was that when people gave their spiritual allegiance to King Jesus, they started opting out of the Roman Zeitgeist and its political and economic systems. Recall what happened in Ephesus. The new converts of the Jesus movement began opting out of huge swaths of the Ephesian economy. Both the magic and idol trades—big, big business in the Roman economy—were disrupted. The riot started when the economic leaders of the city framed the problem as *patriotic* in nature, as an assault on the sacred foundations of their society. The cry that started the riot wasn't

"Rich businessmen are losing money!" but "Great is Artemis of the Ephesians!" The interests of the marketplace were being hidden by patriotic appeals to god and country.

The church was subversive because it challenged and undercut the spiritual idolatry that legitimated an entire economic and political way of life. And when you start chipping away at that foundation the whole building starts to wobble and falter. No wonder riots started breaking out. The church struck a blow at the foundations, and the whole world started to crumble.

The revolutionary nature of the church was that it didn't focus on specific locations of oppression. The church didn't focus on chipping away at a Roman injustice here or a Roman injustice there. The church had a more radical approach—and I use that word intentionally. The word *radical* comes from the Latin word *radix* meaning "root." The church was radical in that it was pulling up the *roots* of Roman society, calling into question the sacred foundations upon which imperial Rome was built. The church challenged the sacred and patriotic truths that justified Roman oppression and the belief that the empire was divinely ordained and, thus, beyond critique. Because, you know, *god* and *country* always go hand in hand. Once again, it's the spiritual *and* the political, two sides of the same coin.

Thus the revolutionary proclamation that Jesus of Nazareth was "Lord of all" (Acts 10:36), even over Caesar. And while Jesus did not consider his *isa Theo* "equal to god" status as something to be taken by force—choosing *kenosis* over *harpagmon*—the Lordship of Jesus did *invalidate* the spiritual legitimacy and authority of Caesar and imperial Rome. Ideologically speaking, Christianity made the empire subject to critique and dissent. Once Christ was confessed as Lord, blind obedience to empire was no longer automatic and assumed. Christianity had shrunk empire down to size. The emperor, the Christians pointed out, had no clothes. And standing naked and exposed before the eyes of their subjects, the empires of the world, then as now, lashed out.

This is why the Romans coined a word to describe the early Christians. The Romans called the early Christians *atheists*—people who denied the gods of the empire, people who rejected the sacred foundations upon which their society had been built. And while the early church might have been nonviolent, this *spiritual revolt and revolution* made them dangerous.

The ironic trouble with political activism is that it is often not radical enough. You might throw a brick through a window, but the principalities and powers can handle a bit of broken glass. And far too often political activism is co-opted by the very powers it is trying to change. Activism often involves fighting empire with the tools of empire, leaving empire fully intact once the marching and protests are over. The status quo remains sturdily in place.

This isn't to say that political activism or electoral politics are useless or ineffective. Some laws and policies are better than others. And some have lasting and revolutionary significance. So it's our duty and responsibility to engage in this ongoing work. But this political work often fails to get to the spiritual roots of systemic injustice and oppression, the sacred and unquestioned values that justify and perpetuate the political and economic systems of the world. Until the gods of the nation are called into question, radical change is not possible. Economics is always about exorcisms.

At the heart of the biblical imagination, the sin at the core of all sin is the sin of *idolatry*, worshiping and giving ultimate allegiance to the god of your nation. Oppression and injustice flow out of this idolatry.

But the nation isn't the only principality and power that's tempting us into idolatry. There are other false gods in the world that make it difficult for us to love each other.

Idols Big and Small

Every moment of every day we are surrounded by a multitude of institutions and organizations that compete for our service, loyalty, attention, allegiance, commitment, and worship. Maybe the nation-state is the Big Idol on the block, but we struggle with lesser idols on a constant and daily basis. The most obvious one is likely to be your place of work. Or any other institution you feel passionate about or committed to. And that includes your religious denomination and church. These are all powers that demand idolatrous loyalty and service, drawing us away from the kingdom of God.

That might sound vague, so let me give some examples. I'm an American. I also root for the San Antonio Spurs. I work for Abilene Christian University as professor and chair of the Psychology Department. I am a man. I am Caucasian. My son plays football for Abilene Christian School. *Go Panthers!* I'm a Christian, a member of the Churches of Christ, and I attend the Highland Church of Christ in Abilene, Texas. I'm also "Richard Beck," a little institution myself, a brand as an author, speaker, and someone with a social media following. And moment by moment I'm tempted in all sorts of ways to privilege service and allegiance to any of these powers over my allegiance to the kingdom of God.

And what I mean by that is that my allegiance and investment in these powers makes it hard for me to love people.

For example, after 9/11 my patriotic buttons got pushed, making it hard to love some people. As a Spurs fan, when Ray Allen of the Miami Heat hit a three-pointer at the end of regulation in Game Six of the 2013 NBA Finals, I had a hard time loving some people. Ray Allen in particular. When a kid hurts my son with a dirty hit in a football game I have a hard time loving some people. At my university when other departments get funds or resources that my department should rightfully have I have a hard time loving some people. When my candidate loses a Presidential election I have a hard time loving some people. When someone spreads a vision of Christianity very different from my own I have a hard time loving some people. And finally, whenever someone pans my book in an Amazon review or criticizes me in the comments section of my blog—well, you guessed it—I have a hard time loving some people.

This is how *worship* is connected to our ability to *love*. When we give our ultimate allegiance to any of the principalities and powers, large or small, we find ourselves perennially at war with anyone who places these things at risk. Idolatry breeds perpetual vigilance and violence.

All of this is simply to say that the confession that *Jesus is Lord of all* turns the world upside down. But much closer to home, that confession turns *my* world upside down. Idolatry isn't just about the nation-state. The kingdom of God uproots all the idols of my life, petty and great.

No wonder riots broke out in city after city when Jesus was proclaimed as Lord of all.

The entire world—my world and your world—was being turned upside down.

Chapter 16

Satan Interrupted

"WE ARE YOUR bad conscience."

At the height of the Nazi nightmare, while millions of Jews were being killed in the extermination camps, mimeographed pamphlets appeared across Germany. The leaflets were written by a group calling themselves the White Rose, and they tried to rouse their fellow citizens from their spiritual and moral slumber. Hitler, the White Rose declared, was a monster who was leading Germany deeper into darkness. In Leaflet No. 4 the White Rose explicitly framed the struggle against Hitler in spiritual and moral terms. Their words scream:

> Every word that proceeds from Hitler's mouth is a lie. When he says peace, he means war. And when he names the name of the Almighty in a most blasphemous manner, he means the almighty evil one, that fallen angel, Satan . . .
>
> We will not keep silent. We are your bad conscience. The White Rose will not leave you in peace![1]

---

1. *"The White Rose Leaflets" Revolt & Resistance.* www.HolocaustResearch Project.org. 10 Dec. 2015.

These words constituted high treason. Whoever the White Rose was, they were flirting with death.

Now widely revered as heroes in Germany, the White Rose was a handful of students from the University of Munich, most of them Christian. And among the leaders of the White Rose were a brother and sister, Hans and Sophie Scholl.[2]

On February 18, 1943 the Scholl siblings were observed distributing what would become known as Leaflet No. 6 of the White Rose on the campus of the University of Munich. They were arrested and quickly brought to a trial presided over by Roland Freisler, one of the most notorious of the Nazi hanging judges. Standing before the Nazi court, both Hans and Sophie remained defiant. Addressing the court, Sophie Scholl said, "Somebody, after all, had to make a start. What we wrote and said is also believed by many others. They just don't dare express themselves as we did."

The Scholls were quickly declared guilty of treason and sentenced to death. The Nazis didn't waste any time. The execution was scheduled to take place that very day. Sophie Scholl's cellmate preserved her final words before she left to face the guillotine:

> How can we expect righteousness to prevail when there is hardly anyone willing to give himself up individually to a righteous cause?

On February 22, 1943 at 5:00 pm, Hans and Sophie Scholl were beheaded by the Nazis. Later, six other members of the White Rose were arrested and executed by the Nazis.

But the words of the White Rose lived on. The final leaflet of the White Rose, Leaflet No. 6, had been smuggled out of Germany and had reached the Allies. Thousands of copies were made and in July 1943, Allied planes dropped the leaflets from the skies over Germany. The defiant words of the White Rose falling down on Nazi Germany like rain.

---

2. Annette E. Dumbach and Jud Newborn, *Sophie Scholl and the White Rose*, revised, expanded edition (Oxford: Oneworld, 2006).

A Resistance of Small Efforts

When the American lawyer and theologian William Stringfellow visited Europe after World War II he spent time visiting with members of various resistance movements, the people who, like the White Rose and Dietrich Bonheoffer, worked to undermine the Nazi regime. What puzzled Stringfellow as he interviewed members of the resistance is how the risks they took seemed to vastly outweigh any progress their small acts of defiance would accomplish. Beyond their leaflets, the White Rose also sprayed anti-Nazi graffiti on the walls of their university and if they had been caught it would have surely led to a death sentence. The risks the White Rose took in spraying that graffiti were enormous. And yet, did they really think anti-Nazi graffiti was going to bring down the Third Reich or stop the ovens burning at Auschwitz?

The risks they took far outweighed the potential for success. Such acts of resistance were small and ineffective. As Stringfellow observed:

> [T]he Resistance . . . consisted, day after day, of small efforts. . . . To calculate their actions—abetting escapes, circulating mimeographed news, hiding fugitives, obtaining money or needed documents, engaging in various forms of noncooperation with the occupying authorities or the quisling bureaucrats, wearing armbands, disrupting official communications—in terms of odds against the Nazi efficiency and power and violence and vindictiveness would seem to render their witness ridiculous. The risks for them of persecution, arrest, torture, confinement, death were so disproportionate to any concrete results that could practically be expected. . . . Yet these persons persevered in their audacious, extemporaneous, fragile, puny, foolish Resistance.[3]

---

3. William Stringfellow, *An Ethic for Christians and Other Aliens in a Strange Land* (Waco, TX: Word, 1973), 118–19.

So why did they persevere? The answer that Stringfellow got was that in a world controlled by the Nazis, resistance was the only way to preserve and protect your humanity. The goal of resistance wasn't simply to topple Hitler. Resistance had to be a way of life, the only way to live as an agent of grace and love in a dark and evil world. To not resist was to die, to undergo to *a spiritual death*, to surrender to the surrounding and enveloping darkness. "Resistance," Stringfellow concluded after his interviews with the resistance movement, "became the only human way to live." And if that meant risking death, well, that was the price for living humanly and humanely in Hitler's Germany. To not resist was to suffer the death of your humanity. A death before death, becoming a moral and spiritual zombie.

As idealistic college students the White Rose probably believed that their leafleting and graffiti efforts were going to make a difference in stopping the war. Perhaps those hopes were not very realistic, but I think we can be sure of one thing: the White Rose *had* to print those leaflets. Resistance was a moral and spiritual imperative. Resistance was the only way the White Rose could live as human beings in the world Hitler had created, the only way to live as human beings who loved themselves and their neighbors.

The Acid of Compassion

In a world dominated by indifference, suffering, and violence, love is a heroic act of resistance.

Spiritual warfare is maintaining this posture of resistance in the face of suffering and evil. And yet, when it comes to spiritual warfare many doubting and disenchanted Christians struggle to maintain the fighting posture of the White Rose. Our compassion pulls us into the suffering of the world, but compassion places a heavy burden upon our faith. The realities of evil and suffering create strong cross-pressures, pressures that can crack, erode, and wash away the foundations of faith.

On the one hand, the alleviation of suffering of the world, through acts of justice and liberation, is the animating force for many Christians. When we envision the Jesus of the Gospels, we thrill to the vision of Jesus lifting up the weak, marginalized, and discarded, the Jesus who was a friend of sinners and prostitutes.

But on the other hand, the problem of evil and suffering in the world is also the very thing that undermines and erodes the faith of so many Christians. I've had many conversations with former Christians who've become atheists or agnostics—too many conversations to even count. And the number one reason for this loss of faith, in conversation after conversation, is the problem of evil and suffering. Why, they ask, if God is loving and powerful, is there so much horrific suffering and pain in the world?

Such are the emotional and theological cross-pressures we feel within our hearts, gale-force winds blowing in completely opposite directions. Suffering *energizing* faith. Suffering *undermining* faith. Both at the same time. This, and I've seen it time and time again, is the great irony and tragedy of how our *compassion* becomes the *acid* that erodes our faith. For many Christians, emulating the *love* of Jesus becomes what erodes *faith* in Jesus.

If a compassionate, justice-focused Christianity is to become a viable expression of the Christian faith, these cross-pressures have to reconciled. And the effects of persistent doubt and disenchantment don't make things any easier.

Bring On the Apocalypse!

But for the White Rose the Holocaust wasn't a theological problem to be solved. For the White Rose the Holocaust was a reality to be resisted. The White Rose embodied what Greg Boyd calls "a theology of revolt."[4] Our response to suffering isn't *intellectual* but *behavioral*. Our response to suffering isn't theological debate and mental rumination—a big pile of questions, doubts, and existential breakdowns. Following the White Rose, our response must be *action*. Resistance is our only theodicy.

---

4. Gregory A. Boyd, *God at War: The Bible & Spiritual Conflict* (Downers Grove, IL: InterVarsity, 1997).

When you adopt a posture of resistance you don't spend time spinning intellectual wheels about the origins of suffering and evil. You take action by stepping into the biblical drama of God's invasion of the cosmos with love. Which is to say that you embrace the Bible's *apocalyptic* approach to "the problem of evil."

Now when you hear the word "apocalypse," you probably think of a cataclysmic event that brings about the end of the world. But the Greek word *apocalypse* simply means "unveiling," as in "to reveal something." And in the hands of the New Testament writers, especially the apostle Paul, the Great Apocalypse in the history of the world isn't about the destruction of the world at the end of time. The Great Apocalypse is the apocalypse *of Jesus Christ*, God breaking into, invading, and disrupting the settled order of the world by establishing the kingdom of God on earth through the Lordship of Jesus.

For example, in his letters Paul states that he received his gospel as an "apocalypse of Jesus Christ," as a revelation that was given to him. And when Paul describes his experience of this apocalypse he describes his Damascus road experience, when Jesus appeared to him, blinding him and knocking him to the ground. The apocalypse of Jesus Christ is something that enters your world and knocks you off your feet The apocalypse of Jesus Christ invades, interrupts, and disrupts Paul's world.

So when we speak about the *apocalyptic* nature of the Bible's approach to "the problem of evil" we are describing *the invasive, interrupting action of God's kingdom breaking into the world through Jesus Christ.*[5] Our posture of resistance is rooted in this apocalyptic understanding of the kingdom of God. Taking a cue from Jesus and the White Rose, we *invade* and *interrupt* the world with love.

---

5. Importantly, it's the apocalyptic nature of the kingdom that allows us to dismiss any charges of metaphysical dualism when speaking about spiritual warfare, that the forces of Light and Darkness are co-equal and eternally pitted against each other. The kingdom of God is experienced as *warfare* because of God's apocalyptic *invasion* of the world, the kingdom being inserted and establishing a foothold in hostile territory.

And that's a critical point. This invasion is the War of the Lamb. The apocalyptic kingdom is *an invasion of love.*

When he was tempted on the mountaintop by Satan, Jesus faced a fork in the road, a decision about how his kingdom would establish a foothold and a beachhead. Satan was the ruler of the world and Jesus was about to invade. At that fork in the road Jesus chose *kenosis* over *harpagmon.* The kingdom of God would not invade or reign using the tools of Satan. The "rule" of the kingdom of God would be *kenarchy*—the rule of love—where the King serves and gives his life away as a ransom for many.

And so Jesus' apocalyptic invasion of the world began. The kingdom of God broke into the world. When you see me casting out demons, Jesus said, you know the kingdom of God has come upon you. The battle had been joined.

A Great Campaign of Sabotage

When we come to embrace Jesus's apocalyptic invasion of the world with love, we begin to appreciate the *tactical* nature of spiritual warfare.

To understand this we need to contrast "tactics" with "strategies."[6] Strategies are techniques used by the powerful. These are the techniques of top-down power and lording over others. Invade, defeat, dominate, expand. Rinse and repeat.

Strategies are the techniques of empire. Strategies are the techniques of *harpagmon* and the Lucifer effect. Strategies are what Satan offered to Jesus on the mountain. The powerful rule the world, Jesus said, by lording over and exercising authority over others.

Tactics, by contrast, are the techniques of the weak. Lacking power and therefore unable to dominate, control, or force things, the weak must resort to the techniques of subversion, sabotage, and

---

6. This contrast between tactics and strategies is taken from Michel de Certeau, *The Practice of Everyday Life,* trans. Steven Rendall (Berkeley: University of California Press, 1984).

guerilla warfare. If strategies are exercises in top-down power, tactics emerge from the bottom up. Further, the weak are always operating in enemy territory. Consequently, the weak have to be opportunistic and experts of improvisation.

Love looks like weakness in the world. Like the Men in White told me out at the prison, meekness is taken for weakness in the world. "You can't do that stuff in here." Or anywhere.

But it's through the weakness of love that God's power is revealed. That is the triumph of the Lamb in Revelation, the subversive victory of the cross over the principalities and powers. As Paul declares in 1 Corinthians 1:27, "God chose the weak things of the world to shame the strong."

And because love appears to us as weakness in the world, love always operates tactically, subversively, and opportunistically. Love doesn't dominate us. Love interrupts us.

Jesus rejected *the strategies of Satan* on the mountain to embrace *the tactics of love*: healing the sick; preaching the good news to the poor; welcoming the unclean; lifting up the oppressed. Jesus didn't conquer, dominate, and control. Jesus invaded and interrupted. As Peter summed it up, Jesus' approach was tactical and opportunistic: He went about doing good and healing all those under the power of the devil.

And these were the same tactics the church employed to turn the world upside down.

In *Mere Christianity*, C. S. Lewis summed it up well:

Enemy-occupied territory—that is what this world is. Christianity is the story of how the rightful king has landed, you might say landed in disguise, and is calling us to take part in a great campaign of sabotage.

There it is, the whole vision of spiritual warfare, the apocalyptic and tactical elements of our theology of revolt. In Jesus the kingdom of God has *apocalyptically* invaded the world, and as this is an invasion of love it's *a tactical engagement*. Love is guerilla warfare. A great campaign of sabotage.

And if that sounds too technical and abstract, I think St. John of the Cross summed up the whole thing rather well:

Where there is no love, put love.

We put love in the world—we insert and invade—where there is no love. *Love is an apocalypse*, our world being tactically interrupted by the surprising, unanticipated experience of grace.

Spiritual warfare is the tactical interruption of the world with love.

Angelic Troublemaking

Given the apocalyptic and tactical nature of the kingdom, spiritual warfare is inherently a *creative* and *situational* expression. Like the anti-Nazi resistance efforts, spiritual warfare is often comprised of small and daily acts of resistance to live humanly in an inhuman world. Love subverts and sabotages the pattern of the world, playfully, innovatively, theatrically, extemporaneously, spontaneously, opportunistically, and artistically. So there are no prototypical or standard visions of what it all should look like. You will only be limited by your imagination and the constraints of love.

But a few practical examples might prove helpful.

When politically focused, interrupting the world with love will often look like "angelic troublemaking," to borrow a phrase from the civil rights activist Bayard Rustin.[7] We've already seen an example of angelic troublemaking with the White Rose and the German resistance movement. The White Rose leaflets interrupted the moral complacency of Nazi Germany, declaring "We will be your bad conscience!" The leaflets were also a form of tactical sabotage.

Another political example of interrupting the world with love comes from the subversive street liturgy described by William

---

7. A. Terrance Wiley, *Angelic Troublemakers: Religion and Anarchism in America* (New York: Bloomsbury Academic, 2014), 107.

Cavanaugh in his book *Torture and Eucharist*.[8] Seeking to expose the torture taking place under the Pinochet regime in Chile, members of the Sebastian Acevedo Movement against Torture would appear in a public place, perform a subversive act of liturgy, and then melt away. These were "flash mobs" that were apocalyptic and tactical acts of love, attempts to interrupt Chilean citizens and the Pinochet regime by drawing attention to human rights abuses. Let me quote Cavanaugh as he describes an example of what one of these "flash mobs" looked like:

> On September 14, 1983, a group of seventy nuns, priests, and laypeople appeared suddenly in front of the CNI clandestine prison at 1470 Borgono Street in Santiago [where most of the torture occurred] and unfurled a banner: A MAN IS BEING TORTURED HERE. They blocked traffic, read a litany of regime abuses, handed out leaflets signed "Movement against Torture," and sang.[9]

Before Pinochet's thugs could arrive to make arrests, the group would disperse and disappear. Subversive street liturgy such as this is a powerful illustration of tactically interrupting the world with love.

As illustrated by the Chilean street liturgy, one of the most important ways we can interrupt the world with love is by simply speaking up and telling the truth. That is what unfurling the banner "A MAN IS BEING TORTURED HERE" did: it told the truth, interrupting lies, falsehoods, propaganda, and illusions. Satan is described in the Bible as the "Father of Lies" (John 8:44). And we are also told that Satan "disguises himself as an angel of light" (2 Corinthians 11:14). More often than not, spiritual warfare is simply telling the truth, especially speaking "truth to power" in the face of the Orwellian propaganda being spread by the principalities and powers.

---

8. William T. Cavanaugh, *Torture and Eucharist: Theology, Politics, and the Body of Christ* (Oxford: Blackwell, 1998).
9. Ibid., 273.

Lovingly interrupting the world with truth is important because exploitative and oppressive power structures are often supported by an ideology buttressed by lies and propaganda. Dispelling the ideological illusions being spun by the principalities and powers is often the first step in tactical interruption. This was what the White Rose was doing with their leaflets. In the words of Václav Havel from his essay "The Power of the Powerless," by accepting Nazi ideology German citizens had come to "live within a lie."[10] While most German citizens did not participate in the extermination of the Jews, the same way most Chileans did not participate in Pinochet's torture program, when we remain silent in the face of injustice and oppression we give aid and support to oppressive and unjust power structures, because our quiet acceptance of the status quo reinforces the status quo as both normal and right. Our silence—our refusal to interrupt our neighbors with truth—is taken as tacit approval of how the powers are running the world. That collective silence creates the illusion of universal agreement and approval, which stifles dissent and protest by making them seem abnormal and crazy.

Lovingly interrupting the world with truth means dispelling the illusion of universal approval and agreement so that dissent and protest can appear sane, reasonable, and legitimate. Simply speaking up makes a difference. Speaking up cracks the illusion of universal agreement, making dissent and protest possible. A new way of life becomes imaginable. Speaking up is angelic troublemaking, lovingly interrupting the world with truth.

So these, then, are some political examples of "angelic troublemaking." Large and risky acts of subversion, from the White Rose leaflets and subversive street liturgy, to smaller but still significant acts of resistance, like speaking up and speaking the truth when others remain silent.

---

10. Václav Havel, *The Power of the Powerless: Citizens against the State in Central-eastern Europe* (Armonk, NY: M.E. Sharpe, 1985).

Interrupting the World with Love

There are less political ways we can interrupt the world with love. Especially as we stand in the face of suffering, trauma, and loss.

One of my favorite examples of this are the vigils for murder victims described by Marcia Owen in her book with Samuel Wells, *Living Without Enemies: Being Present in the Midst of Violence.*[11] Owen is a member of the Religious Coalition for a Nonviolent Durham, a group formed to address the plague of gun violence in Durham, North Carolina. Owen tells the story of how in the early days of the RCND their work was focused on political activism, mainly advocacy efforts to get gun control legislation passed. But as the years passed the most profound and transformative work that the RCND found itself engaged with was organizing prayer vigils at the location where people had been murdered by gun violence in Durham. This has been a shift in the RCND away from *policy* to *solidarity*, from a "working for" model of engagement to a "being with" model of engagement, standing in solidarity with those who are suffering in the world. The heart of the prayer vigils involves inviting the family and loved ones of the victim to gather with neighbors and community members at the site of the murder for a time of shared silence, lament, prayer, and remembrance. As Owen and Wells write, "Prayer vigils are a ministry of presence and place, rather than of performance. . . . The aim is to recognize publicly the human worth of the victim and perpetrator, to comfort family and friends and to sanctify and bring healing to the site where the violence occurred. A vigil requests nothing more than willingness to be present and receptive to God's mercy."[12]

The Durham prayer vigils for murder victims don't solve anything politically. They don't bring the dead person back to life or make the pain of the family go away. But the vigils have been a profound

---

11. Samuel Wells and Marcia A. Owen, *Living Without Enemies: Being Present in the Midst of Violence* (Downers Grove, IL: InterVarsity, 2011).
12. Ibid., 75.

source of healing and reconciliation in Durham, for the families who have lost loved ones, for the perpetrators, for the neighborhoods, and for the city. The prayer vigils have interrupted the violence of Durham and have brought healing to those who are suffering.

Beyond interrupting the world through resistance and solidarity, we can also interrupt the world with acts of inclusion and kindness. If Jesus had a favorite tactic it was his practice of table fellowship, breaking bread with the outcasts of society.

A few years ago my friend Colby Martin and I did a church retreat together. In the final talk at the retreat I was speaking about the topic of this chapter, about how spiritual warfare is interrupting the world with love.

After the final talk on the last day of the retreat Colby wanted to send the church home with homework. He broke everyone up into groups and asked them to come up with a plan to "subvert the world" by doing creative, beautiful, and loving things, individually or together, in the weeks to come.

A few weeks after the retreat Colby got an email from a church member reporting back about the retreat challenge to go out and creatively subvert the world with love:

O.K., I have a story for you.

At the retreat our small group decided we would each do something towards reaching our assignment's goal.

I decided I would make and distribute PB&J sandwiches. They're high in protein, soft and crunchy at the same time and I just love them!

Let me back up, I work downtown in one of the nicest buildings. Even the lobby is scented.

Anyway, I can walk in any direction on any given day and I will encounter a number of homeless people. What an opportunity to feed someone a little something by only taking a few steps!

So between conference calls today, I whipped up six sandwiches and headed outside. I gave them all out within minutes to people who immediately introduced themselves to me by name.

No longer were they people sitting cross legged on the sidewalk holding a sign, they were all God's children and I connected with each of them one on one.

Now the best part . . . I had three sandwiches left in my polka dot covered party bag. I saw three guys standing at a trashcan talking. I walked up, introduced myself and offered them each a sandwich.

They were all appreciative and the tallest guy said his name was Chris. He had pink skin and steel blue eyes. He said it was his birthday!

I wished him a Happy Birthday and turned to walk back to my office. I was three feet off the ground. I am STILL emotional about it. How easy was that? How awesome is that?

I love this story because it illustrates *exactly* how the apocalyptic interruption of the world with love is often creative, extemporaneous, improvisational, spontaneous, theatrical, and opportunistic.

Spiritual warfare is putting love where there is no love. It is the action of grace in territory controlled by the devil, being true to love in a world that is cold and lonely and mean. It is the kingdom of God breaking into and interrupting our lives.

Spiritual warfare is leaflets falling from the sky, graffiti on a wall, flash mob street liturgy, and speaking the truth.

Spiritual warfare is the prayer vigil on a blood-soaked city sidewalk and giving up a prestigious educational position to teach history at an inner-city High School.

Spiritual warfare is facing a beating when you step out of a gang, counting your blessings, and singing in the darkness.

Spiritual warfare is prayer, worship, holiness, discerning the spirits, and the liturgy of drinking bad coffee together.

Spiritual warfare is a polka-dot-covered party bag filled with peanut butter sandwiches.

Spiritual warfare is this, and a million other things. Spiritual warfare is Satan interrupted.

It is the kingdom of God's great campaign of sabotage.

EPILOGUE:
A PRISON STORY

AS I'VE SAID, I was reintroduced to the Devil in prison.

I say reintroduced because having grown up in the church, I'd met the Devil a long time ago as a child. But my faith tradition wasn't charismatic or Pentecostal, so we didn't talk about the Devil all that much. I knew who the Devil was, we'd been introduced, but I didn't think or worry about him all that much.

I mostly worried about God. As I got older and moved into my college years my questions about faith grew in both number and intensity. And as my doubts grew I focused more and more intensely upon God. What was God doing in the world? Did God answer prayer? Why did God allow the Holocaust to happen, along with a million other evil things too horrible to imagine?

Did God even exist?

The more I thought about God the less I thought about the Devil. The Devil, as an article of faith, was just something I couldn't afford to waste time or energy on. The existence of the Devil? I had bigger theological fish to fry.

Added to this was the fact that I've never had a single experience of the occult. I've never caught the scent of brimstone, never encountered an evil presence that disturbed me or shook me to the core. And having worked for many years in a psychiatric hospital I've seen just about everything that can be seen when it comes to human behavior. I've seen some pretty weird stuff. But I've never seen anything that I would consider to be demon possession.

As best I can tell, the Devil and I and have never met face to face.

But I do know people who've met the Devil and who have seen demon possessions and exorcisms. I've listened with an open mind to their stories and experiences. I don't doubt them. But I am one of those people who always withholds judgment until I have firsthand experience. I'm sort of like Thomas the apostle in that way. I have to see things with my own eyes.

And so, well into my forties, my faith didn't have much room for the Devil. I hardly ever thought about him, let alone spoke about him.

And then a few years ago I started teaching the Bible study out at the maximum-security prison north of town. And there the Devil and I were reintroduced.

The Men in White spoke about the Devil all the time. And as I listened I tried to process and translate as best I could. As I said, I'd never given the Devil much thought, wasn't raised in a charismatic or Pentecostal church, and had never had any personal experiences with demons. But the men were describing *something* to me, something they named as the Devil or Satan or as demonic. And every week I worked hard to catch a glimpse of the shape of what that something might be.

As I've recounted, my first glimpse of the Devil out at the prison occurred when we reached the Beatitudes in the Sermon on the Mount. "In here," they said, "meekness is taken for weakness. You can't do that stuff in here. You'll get hurt."

That night the Devil and I were officially reintroduced.

When I listened to the men, that day and since, as they described their day-to-day struggles, I began to trace the shape of the Devil out at the prison. No, I didn't see horns and a pitchfork, but I began to discern the shape of that something the men were always talking about.

There was a force pressing down upon the men, a brutal, violent, and dehumanizing force. In the Bible it's called "the pattern of this world," a world ruled by the prince of the power of the air. That night I began to discern what was happening to the souls of the men. They felt that something was pressing down upon them, something trying to force them into, to squeeze them into, the brutal, violent, and dehumanizing shape that conformed to the world they were living in. That force was everywhere, pressing down, down, down upon them. Tempting them. Taunting them. Demoralizing them. Yelling at them. Whispering to them. Squeezing the life out of them. A force working tirelessly to mold them into its dark image. And if not to mold them, then to break them. To walk them through despair to suicide.

I don't know if this force is consciously *malevolent*, but it is most definitely *malignant*. And really, it doesn't much matter which it is. Because more than anything, the force is *real*.

As I left the Bible study that night I was pretty shaken. I had looked into the darkness of the world inside the prison and realized just how insane the Beatitudes sounded.

Weeks passed and we found ourselves reading the story of Jesus washing the disciples' feet. And as I read the story to the class, looks of skepticism came over their faces again, the same looks I saw when we were reading the Beatitudes.

Once again, I stopped reading.

"The look on your faces tells me," I said, "that you're not buying any of this."

And so we revisited our previous conversation. Once again I was reintroduced to the Devil, hearing story after story of the dark, violent, and dehumanizing force pressing down upon the men, saturating the atmosphere like an oppressive fog.

But this time I wanted to push harder than I had before. I was looking for answers. Not just for the men, but for myself. Can the cruciform way of Jesus be lived out in this world? Even in a prison?

So I pressed forward.

"Have you ever acted," I asked, "as Jesus acts in this story?"

There was a long silence.

Then one man, Mr. Garcia, raised his hand.

I was intrigued, wondering what Mr. Garcia would say. Mr. Garcia is a big, intimidating man who could snap me like a twig. He commands a lot of respect from the other men.

I called on Mr. Garcia and, given his intimidating presence, figured he'd repeat the "you can't do that in here" consensus.

Mr. Garcia began, speaking softly.

"Well," he started with his heavy Hispanic accent, "I don't know if this is what you are looking for, but I help my cellmate."

"How?" I asked.

"Well, my celly isn't too bright. Something is wrong with his head. He was in an accident so he's not too smart."

The men in the study who know Mr. Garcia's cellmate nod in agreement and elaborate. Apparently, as I pieced it together from what they described to me, Mr. Garcia's cellmate has a cognitive disability and requires a lot of help taking care of himself and navigating prison life.

Mr. Garcia continued.

"Well, when my celly first got put in with me I noticed that he never took off his shoes. He always left them on. So one day I finally asked him, 'Why don't you ever take off your shoes?' He wouldn't tell me. Weeks and months passed and he never took off his shoes. Never."

This makes all of us cringe. Texas prisons are not air-conditioned and in the summer the temperatures reach 100 degrees for weeks on end. The prison becomes an oven. And if you *never* took off your shoes, not even to shower, sweating as the men do? What must his feet look and smell like?

"After months," Mr. Garcia went on, "finally I got him to tell me why he never took off his shoes. He was embarrassed. He didn't know how to take care of his feet. So his toenails were all overgrown, smelly and ugly looking."

Mr. Garcia paused, and you could hear a pin drop.

"So I asked him to take off his shoes and socks. And his nails were awful. The smell was terrible. But he didn't know how to cut his nails.

"So I sat him down and had him put his feet in a pan of warm water. Then I took his foot in my lap and cut his toenails for him. Showing him how. I don't know what people would have thought if they walked by our cell, his foot in my lap like that. I would never have thought I'd be doing something like that. But I cut his toenails for him."

When Mr. Garcia finished there was a deep silence in the room. The image before us was so surprising and unexpected. Here was this huge, intimidating man taking the time, tender as a mother, to gently wash the feet and trim the disgusting toenails of his mentally disabled cellmate.

Yes, I was reintroduced to the Devil out at the prison. But that night, when Mr. Garcia shared his story, I was also reintroduced to the kingdom of God. That's the night I started believing in spiritual warfare. When Mr. Garcia told that story I saw clearly what it looked like to say, "Get behind me, Satan!" in the prison and in the world.

I saw that night what it looks like to interrupt the world with love. In the words of Flannery O'Connor, I'd seen the action of grace in territory controlled by the devil.

Breaking the silence, Mr. Garcia looked up at me and asked, "Is that an example of what you are talking about?"

I smiled and nodded, my eyes suddenly moist.

"Yes," I said, "that is an example of what I'm talking about."

ACKNOWLEDGMENTS

I'd like to extend a warm thank you to Fortress Press and Theology for the People for the kind invitation to write this book. And a special Thank You to Tony Jones for all his editorial work and advice. Plus, the seeds of this book were planted many years ago when Tony challenged progressive Christians on his blog to articulate a positive and compelling vision of the Christian faith. Thank you, Tony, for the challenge and all your help and encouragement.

I would also like to thank Mark Love, Matt Dabbs, Stephen Backhouse, Roger Mitchell, Colby Martin, Greg Boyd, and Brad East for conversations and ideas that shaped this book. And to the kind and thoughtful readers of my blog *Experimental Theology* for all their input and insights when I first shared some of this material on my blog—Thank you.

This book is dedicated to the Men in White, the inmates at the French-Robertson Unit who attend the Monday-night Bible study led by Herb Patterson and myself, and to my brothers and sisters at Freedom Fellowship. I am not exaggerating when I say that the Men in White and the saints at Freedom saved my faith. I hope my love and gratitude for them shines through the pages of this book. And a big Thank You to Herb, my dear brother, for introducing me to "Old Scratch" and for the years we've partnered together to serve the Men in White.

Finally, I'd like to thank my family.

Brenden and Aidan, I love you. The world might be cold, lonely, and mean but the love we share warms and protects us. Carry that love into the world, boys, and welcome others into it.

And Jana, you know exactly what I'm going to say:

There is love.

Always.